Making Wood Decks, Fences & Gates

•••••

Charles R. Self, L. O. Anderson,
T. B. Heebink & A. E. Oviatt

 Sterling Publishing Co., Inc.   New York

This book is dedicated in loving memory to Faith Fitch Hill, the mother of three fine people, a friend who was an original, and the antithesis of the mother-in-law found in many jokes.

She was an intelligent, caring, and superb person. Her recent death takes a large portion of light from my life and from the lives of her children and grandchildren.

Library of Congress Cataloging-in-Publication Data

Making wood decks, fences & gates / Charles R. Self . . . [et al.].
    p.   cm.
    Includes index.
    ISBN 0-8069-6899-0
    1. Fences—Design and construction.   2. Decks (Architecture, Domestic)—Design and construction.   3. Gates—Design and construction.   4. Building, Wooden.   I. Self, Charles R.
II. Title: Making wood decks, fences and gates.
TH4965.M35   1989
694-dc19   88-38511
                                     CIP

1 3 5 7 9 10 8 6 4 2

Published in 1989 by Sterling Publishing Co., Inc.
Two Park Avenue, New York, N.Y. 10016
The material in this book was originally published
under the titles "Wood Fences & Gates," copyright 1986 by
Charles R. Self, and "Wood Decks," published in 1979 by
Sterling Publishing Co., Inc.
Distributed in Canada by Oak Tree Press Ltd.
% Canadian Manda Group; P.O. Box 920, Station U
Toronto, Ontario, Canada M8Z 5P9
Distributed in Great Britain and Europe by Cassell PLC
Artillery House, Artillery Row, London SW1P 1RT, England
Distributed in Australia by Capricorn Ltd.
P.O. Box 665, Lane Cove, NSW 2066
Manufactured in the United States of America
All rights reserved
Sterling ISBN 0-8069-6899-0 Paper

Contents

Color section follows page 96.

Preface

WOOD FENCES AND GATES

For years I have heard neighbors argue over the sturdiness and styles of various fences. Often, the discussion ends amicably. But occasionally the decision to build even the best fence (from the builder's point of view) may cause ill will.

Certainly, a fence that is improperly designed or built can cause enmity if pets or livestock are not kept under control. Turn loose your cows, horses, sheep, or even worse pigs in a neighbor's grazing, and quite soon you will have problems more costly than the finest fencing.

Residential fences generally serve different purposes and pose problems different from those involving animals. Most often these problems arise because of inappropriate designs—extreme heights, too little setback for codes, and other such items of law or opinion. There is seldom, except for setback and height codes, a factual basis for the dislike, which tends to make the resulting arguments even more emotional.

Fences, regardless of the problems and costs they produce, are an essential part of life in many areas (Illus. 1). For the farmer they serve to protect

Illus. 1. Blue Ridge Parkway post-and-rail fence that was made with double posts.

stock. For the homeowner, fences serve many purposes, including delineating boundaries, decoration, providing privacy, and keeping trespassers out.

In this book I discuss fence styles, materials, tools, and methods for erecting the most practical and popular types. Usually performance and price have to be considered together, or else things get a bit expensive. A very short fence, consisting of one or two or even three panels of privacy screening made from expensive materials, is one thing. But several miles of pasture fencing would require much less expensive materials and a much different design.

DECKS

Outdoor living is becoming a way of life for the American family. Moderate seasons and climates stimulate special enthusiasm for outdoor living. Thus, there is a desire for the outdoor "living room," an area adjacent to the home for family enjoyment in pleasant weather.

This outdoor living area is often provided by a wood deck that adds spaciousness to a home at modest cost (Illus. 2). A deck can expand or frame a view to increase a homeowner's enjoyment. It can serve as an adult entertainment center by night and a children's play area by day—being easily adapted to the activity or degree of formality desired.

Decks, which may offer the only means of providing outdoor living areas for steep hillside homes, have gained popularity for homes on level ground—as a way of adding charm, style, and livability. To achieve these gains, wood decks offer a variety of flexible, economical systems, and this book suggests ways to insure the greatest satisfaction from such systems.

Most of the decks considered here are low- or high-level decks with spaced floor boards and are attached to the house for access and partial support. There are, in addition, detached low-level decks and rooftop decks. The later are simpler than others in some respects since they rely on the roof for primary support but do introduce a need to prevent leakage to the space below. Solid decks may be made of caulked planking or of plywood with a waterproof coating, such as an elastomeric wearing surface.

Low-level wood decks may be chosen for their nonreflective and resilient qualities in preference to a paved patio. More frequently, the wood deck is chosen because of its design versatility and adaptability to varied use.

Low-level decks can be simply supported on concrete piers or short posts closely spaced, thereby simplifying the main horizontal structure. However, drainage can be a problem on low or level ground and provision to insure good drainage should be made before the deck is built. Good drainage not only keeps the ground firm to adequately support the deck but avoids dampness that could encourage decay in posts or sills.

Hillside decks were first in the line of residential decks—used as a means of creating outdoor living areas on steep sites. Despite their expense as compared with a level yard or patio, they add living area at much less cost than that of indoor space. Moreover, the outdoor setting adds a new dimension to the home and provides amenities that people prize.

The substructure of hillside decks is designed to provide solid support with a minimum number of members, especially if exposed to view from below. This may require a heavier deck structure and more substantial railings than are needed for low-level decks, but the general rules to insure satisfactory performance are the same.

Rooftop decks may cover a carport roof or a room of the house. One constructed over a carport may be relatively simple to build but may be difficult to handle aesthetically.

Illus. 2. Sheltered decks extend living areas.

Where a rooftop provides the deck support, it may also serve as the floor, particularly if the deck is included in the initial construction. The roof must then be designed as a floor to support the deck loads. If the deck is added to a completed house, it is more common to construct a separate deck floor over the roof.

A first step in planning a deck is to determine the requirements and limitations of the local building code. Limitations on height and width and required floor loads or railing resistance vary by locality and need to be checked before a deck is designed.

A choice between one large deck and two or more smaller decks may be influenced by code limitations, although the choice is more likely to be based on orientation, view, prevailing winds, steepness of the site, or anticipated desires of the owner.

Deciding deck location goes a long way toward determining the type of deck but leaves a wide choice in design. Where wood is selected as the deck material, there are many design considerations that can contribute to deck durability and enhance the owner's enjoyment of this outdoor living area.

Planning a deck during the design of the house is certainly an advantage because it can then become an outdoor extension of the living or family room. It can also be designed as an outdoor portion of the dining room or kitchen with access through sliding doors or other openings. It is also desirable to take advantage of prevailing breezes with space for both sun and shade areas during the day. Sun shades can be used as a substitute for the natural shade provided by trees.

Providing a deck for an existing house is sometimes more difficult because the rooms may not be located to provide easy access to a deck. However, introduction of a new doorway in the house and a pleasant walkway to the deck area may provide a satisfactory solution to even the most difficult problem.

• • •

Whether you are building wood fences and gates or decks, bear in mind that labor is the heaviest investment. The savings on do-it-yourself work is almost always high enough to offset the cost of the most durable materials for the job.

The intent of this book is to examine the kinds of fences and decks average homeowners can erect either alone or with a little help from their friends. However, if you don't want to take on the work load yourself, there is enough information here for you to become familiar with design and construction, which will make working with a contractor simpler and more satisfying.

FENCES & GATES

1 · Fence Design

Because there are so many uses for fences, design is often the most important step, and it is usually the one most people omit: a fence is needed; a fence is erected. It may serve at least part of its purpose, so the builders leave it up, but it could be dangerous or inefficient. So begin by determining what the fence's function will be and what kind of terrain it must cover. Any fence is somewhat expensive. Although doing it yourself will lower the cost, it will also add quite a bit of work, often quite hard work.

Fence design begins with a definition of its uses. If a privacy screen is required, then the fence may be constructed in one of many shapes and with various materials that prevent a distinct view. If protection is required, a higher fence with stronger, different materials will be needed (Illus. 3).

Illus. 3. Post-and-rail fence is in the foreground, and a tall vertical-board fence is in the background, which serves as a security fence, a wind-break, and a privacy screen.

Horse fencing differs a great deal from cattle fencing, so stock fences are not all alike. (Pig fencing is often the most difficult to construct because the animals love to root.) Decorative fencing around a house depends mostly on your idea of design and the amount of time and money you wish to spend (Illus. 4).

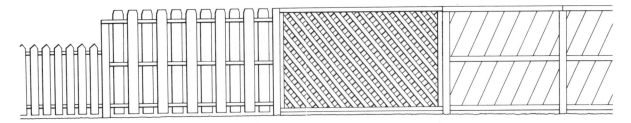

Illus. 4. Common fence types. Left to right: picket, board and board, lattice, panel.

First, then, sit down and define your fence needs or desires. If a fence must serve multiple purposes (Illus. 5) be sure to note them all. Once that's done, look through this book and select a fence that appeals to you, seems to be affordable, and is relatively simple to erect. Incidentally, the longer the fence, the simpler you will want to make the overall design. The reasons

Illus. 5. This decorative fence provides shade, privacy, and wind protection. Built of a less expensive grade of red-wood, Construction Heart, this fence is economical and easy to maintain because of its inherent resistance to insects and decay.

here are cost and time. You can readily understand how complex fence designs for a large farm would be impractical.

So, let's take a look at several types of fences. In many cases, although the materials and construction methods are the same, the actual designs are very, very different.

Fences today have come to mean the more or less airy, light structures made of wood or wire, or of wood, wire, and other materials that we see every day. In the past, stone walls not only a prison made, but also a fence, as you can readily tell by driving through the Middle Atlantic states and up into New York and New England. In those areas, after farmers cut down the trees, they delineated fields with the stones they had plowed up. Today, such structures are classified as walls, not fences, though fences actually are a form of wall.

The requirements for efficiency, strength, and attractiveness of a fence change as the use of the fence changes. Of course, the stronger a fence must be, the more it is likely to cost. There's also a relationship between attractiveness and cost, though not always a direct one. Some of the ugliest security fences in the world are probably also the most expensive, while a fence of rough-sawn boards may be both inexpensive and very attractive. Efficiency is a result of matching cost to use without adding extra features or leaving out needed features (Illus. 6).

General uses for fences include marking property boundaries, keeping people out or in, keeping animals out or in, defining an area (such as pastures or paddocks), providing a privacy screen, providing a windbreak, halting the drift of snow across certain areas, reducing the noise that reaches an area, providing decoration, and determining landscaping limits.

Boundary fences are territorial markers in the truest sense and can be among the cheapest fences to build in terms of materials and labor but the most expensive to keep in terms of lawsuits and zoning restrictions. Boundary fences need only be lightweight, short markers that indicate the limits of your land (Illus. 7), but if proper attention isn't paid to actual property lines and to building codes calling for particular setbacks and other restrictions, all sorts of problems may arise. A boundary fence is also often designed to provide security or privacy (Illus. 8).

Security fencing is usually the most expensive fence style. In truth, it's probably impractical for homeowners to attempt to install the kind of

Illus. 8. Lattice-top board fence of sapwood-streaked Clear grade redwood serves as an inviting enclosure for private outdoor activities.

security fencing that will prevent determined persons from trespassing. First, the expense is horrendous. Second, innocent people could be harmed, which could lead to very expensive lawsuits. As an example, assume you install a diamond-mesh chain-link fence, 10 or 12 feet high with a barbed-wire overhang, and then turn on the electricity and post large warning signs. Well, readily available electric fence transformers are unlikely to do much real damage to a healthy person, but they do smart more than a little when the electrified area is touched. Not too long ago, I was clearing a dead tree from a cattle pasture and happened to back into a single-strand electric fence with one jeans-clad leg. Of course I was damp with sweat, which added to the shock, but take my word for it, it stings. Wiring for an intrusion alarm would make more sense. As for the barbed-wire overhang, these days you will probably have to rip it down because codes disallow it or because you lose a lawsuit filed for destroying the neighborhood's appearance.

A chain-link fence is probably the best choice for security purposes but check first with codes and neighbors to make sure the industrial look won't cause problems. Too, it's probably wise to keep the height under 10 feet and to use something other than the standard metallic-looking materials.

Let's also consider security fences that keep children or small animals *within* a particular area. Such fences need to be just high enough to defeat a small child's attempts at climbing. Again, a chain-link wire fence works well, as do several kinds of board fencing. Height is usually less of a problem with children than with small animals: dogs can usually jump higher.

Animal fencing involves lots of planning for the particular animal. In general, two kinds of animals are difficult to fence for (or against)—goats and horses. Goats seem able to climb anything they want to and to find holes in the fence; horses panic easily, and in their confusion may not see certain types of fencing material, striking it and badly injuring themselves. Cows are easily fenced in or out, but calves less than a year old can make you crazy by getting out through the holes in fences. It has now been only three days since I woke to find my yard covered with calves and a few of their mammas. My landlady had had her animals moved from summer to winter pasture, and the newer infants immediately searched for and found the sections of fence that hadn't been repaired this past summer. Animal fencing, then, requires detailed planning: two- or three-strand barbed wire is fine for cattle but not good for horses, while a single strand of electrified wire, with markers every 6 or 8 feet, will often do very well for horses. (After a few months, you will need to turn the electricity on only once or twice a week as a reminder.)

Privacy screening in crowded suburban areas can be quite important and could possibly assume some importance in residential sections of smaller

Illus. 9. This type of board fencing is excellent for horses.

urban areas. In most cases, privacy screening is made up of fairly tall panels, either of dense plastic or of wood, and placed so it obstructs a direct view of the area being screened out. Many such screens are built today to hide unsightly areas, such as junkyards, from the public eye, and they certainly do tend to improve areas that were once eyesores. Walling in a small yard too tightly may give privacy at the expense of feeling claustrophobic, so try to achieve a balance—alternate solid fencing with more open sections where you may place plantings or different screening structures.

Providing wind control with a fence is not easy. In some areas planting fast-growing trees—even though they take nearly a decade to be effective—might be a better solution. If you do decide to build a fence, first check prevailing wind direction in and around your yard for several seasons, if possible. You may find, though, that although the wind blows in one direction at the front of the house, it comes from an entirely different direction at the rear of the house where you wish to screen it because trees, the house, and other structures toss it around. Wind screens should be made from moderately heavy materials, but it is usually best to develop a design that diffuses instead of blocks the wind. A 45-mile-per-hour wind can rip a goodly chunk of fence down if there's nowhere for it to go except up, while the same wind will shift into a series of gentle breezes if offered numerous outlets in the fence.

Noise-control fences work pretty much the same way, redirecting sound. Very few fence materials absorb sound to any degree, so redirection and reduction is all you can hope for. A very thick fence may seem like a good choice, but if all it does is transfer the noise, it's a waste of money. Probably the best bet is a fence that at least interferes with the sound direction and which is built so that you can plant along it easily. The plants will do the actual muffling. Consider, though, that some experts say it takes a full mile of woodland to cut the noise from a major highway. You may reduce such noise, but you probably won't totally eliminate it.

Decorative fences are some of the most widely used types of fences and choosing one style can be difficult. There are very few restrictions on decorative fencing, although you need to consider construction quality, expense, and local codes. You might want the fence style to complement that of your house and the neighborhood in general, but if you don't wish to do so, then it need not—assuming there are no restrictive covenants in your deed, a neighborhood association agreement, or local building codes.

Once you determine the fence's use, look over a number of fence styles and consider materials before making the plan that will be your final layout. You may have a number of needs in mind (Illus. 10). For example, a fence to keep a riding animal or two enclosed will differ from one used to surround a pasture or to view animals for sale. In the latter case, it becomes almost imperative that the fence be attractive as well as sturdy. The cheaply erected electric fence, therefore, is seldom used if it could be visible to customers.

Materials for decorative fences range in price from free to very expensive. Old wagon wheels found in an abandoned barn make an attractive

Illus. 10. This decorative pool fence serves other purposes as well: it provides security, privacy and protection from the wind.

fence. But if you decide to build a fence out of chestnut, and if you can find any to buy, it would be prohibitively expensive because it is so rare a wood.

The term board fence could be said to refer to every style of fence that requires boards, but more often it refers to a moderately high, to high, fence of boards that are seldom wider than 6 inches (Illus. 11). Board fences are exceptionally popular as stock fencing for horses, because they are so easy to see, even to a panicked animal, and are relatively inexpensive if you use a combination of board and wire-mesh. Cost is a major problem with extensive board fencing, because it requires a great deal of wood, large numbers of nails (or screws), and a lot of labor. In many areas of the country, you can help control the cost by using rough-cut lumber from a local sawmill. As an example of price differences, in my area dried and planed pine today costs about three times what rough, green oak or pine does at several local sawmills.

Picket fences require rails and then pickets that are spaced at intervals along the rails (Illus. 12). Most are well under 6 feet tall, so erection and maintenance are fairly simple, although the actual construction of each fence panel is much more laborious than with post-and-rail fences. Since their main purpose is decorative, pickets may be cut in a wide variety of sizes and styles, fancy or plain. The picket fence offers a number of advantages. First, materials consist of simple boards, and the final design can be simple or complicated, as you desire. Second, the low models outline a property without blocking the view. Third, basic construction is simple, and materials don't have to be exotic. Finally, they contain small children and pets very well.

Rail fences are among the most popular across the country today, for a variety of reasons. Virtually all the designs are easy to erect compared to other types of fences, and for anyone doing a modest amount of fencing,

Illus. 11 (left). This rough-cut vertical-board fence shows how attractive this style can be. Unfortunately, the builder didn't use galvanized or aluminum nails, and even in the dry Arizona weather, the hardware rusted, producing streaks.

Illus. 12 (right). Would you call this a picket fence? I've been told that these ocotillo pickets will often take root, but even if they don't, they are an unusual and attractive relief from the basic wire fence.

the cost of the three most useful materials—redwood, cedar, and pressure-treated woods—are reasonable. Height can be varied to serve several purposes, so that a 3-foot-high two-rail fence makes a nice property-line marker or decorative fence, while a three- or four-rail fence 5 or 6 feet high makes an excellent enclosure for horses or other livestock.

In the South the zigzag (Illus. 13), or snake, fence can still be found, but because it requires so much material and takes up so much space, its primary use today is decorative. When choosing wood for this type of fence, be sure the bottom rails in particular are made of rot-resistant wood, to ensure the fence's longevity.

While today's post-and-rail fence requires holes bored into the posts, the old-time post-and-rail fence—comprised of less material than the zigzag fence—was made with two posts, with rails that were dropped between them and wired in place for added security. The double-post fence is, like the zigzag fence, still an option for those of you who wish to do the entire job from scratch. I've never seen a kit from a factory for either of these

Illus. 13. The snake, or zigzag, fence is found in many areas of the South. This one is on the Blue Ridge Parkway about 30 miles from Roanoke, Virginia.

types, so the job starts with the location of suitable trees and moves from felling them to splitting them and then to building the fences.

Metal fences. In addition to fences made from wood, or mostly wood, are fences made from metal. The most popular is the chain-link fence of galvanized wire. Manufactured with various-colored vinyl coatings, these fences can be constructed with wood or plastic inserts to increase privacy. However, to save money you can make your own inserts.

The basic construction of chain-link fences is the same no matter who supplies the materials. It includes metal posts with caps, the chain-link wire fabric, top rails, various fittings, and usually some sort of torsion device. Cost is fairly high but can be reduced by installing the fence yourself.

Other forms of metal fences abound, and temporary fence types are so numerous as to defy listing. Chicken-wire mesh for gardens, of course, is simple to put up and take down. In most areas, a 2-inch mesh with metal posts driven in to accept a 3- or 4-foot-high fence is fine. Wire fences have been available for a long, long time, and barbed wire is now over 100 years old. Such fences are most suitable for livestock and then only for sheep and cattle.

Once you decide what your fence must do, then decide on an overall plan.

2 ♦ Board and Panel Fences

To prevent confusion, I will define the various types of board fences and look at what a fence panel is as opposed to a panel fence. First, a fence panel is one section of a fence, from post to rail or other filler end (and including a second post if it's an end panel). A panel fence, though, is a fence made of panels, usually plywood but often board, that have been assembled in units, either 2, 4, 6, or 8 feet wide (Illus. 14).

Board fences include almost all types of fence constructed mainly of boards that measure 6″ wide or less. (Wider individual boards tend to warp badly in a relatively short period of time.) With the exception of picket fences, which compose a chapter (page 37) of their own, board-fence designs include those with X-shapes, straight boards, latticework, and basket-

Illus. 14. Step-down fence of Construction Heart redwood graces a gentle slope. Note how stepped panels are formed, and how well the gate is integrated into the design. Construction methods for the basic gate are the same as those covered in Chapter 11, page 107, but require a jigsaw, and your designs drawn in advance for an accurate fit.

weave pattern (often also used in panel fences—see examples in color section). Gate construction for these types of fences is explained in Chapter 11, page 107.

The variations on board-fence designs (Illus. 15, 16) are numerous, and I'm sure I haven't seen them all. If you think of one that better suits your purpose than any discussed here, I suggest you spend an hour or two with an architect's rule and some graph paper to ascertain possible problems. Then go ahead with your own design. There are few secrets in designing a fence. All it requires is a knowledge of what you want the fence to do, some basic arithmetic, and a modest knowledge of the materials to be used. After

Illus. 15. This series of fence designs (also Illus. 16, next page) is an excellent introduction to the many types of board fences.

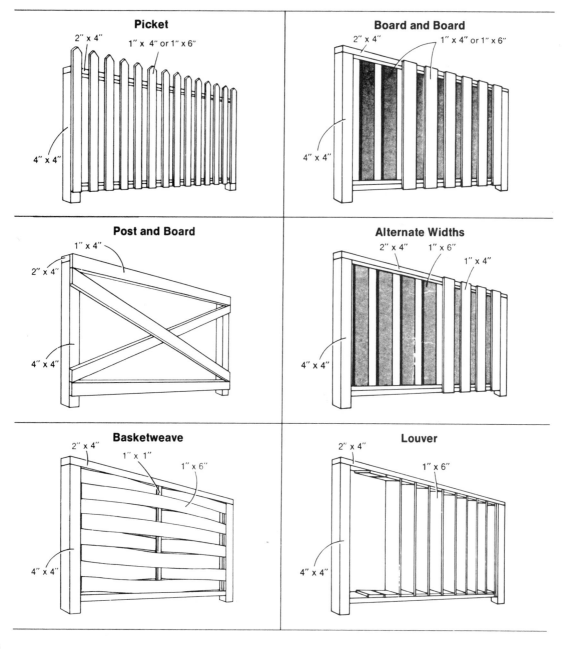

all, fences were erected long before recorded history, and some of today's models probably haven't changed much in basic design since Stone Age man built thornbush confines to keep animals out (or in). After all, what is barbed wire except a man-made thornbush?

So, if you don't see an appealing board fence among the designs here, design your own. Be sure to consider its function (how strong it must be to be effective) and local codes (for setback and fence height). Codes can often be modified if you show a need for a larger, smaller, or closer-to-the-property-line fence (Illus. 17).

Illus. 16.

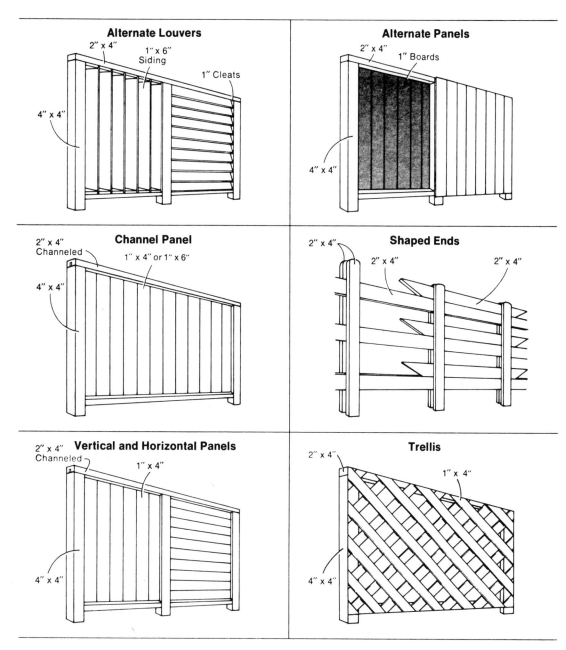

Illus. 17. Construction Heart redwood forms this hillside fence. Note the alternating panel designs, which add interest.

Board-and-board and board-and-batten fences are as attractive as wood siding for buildings, but they are often far easier to construct (requiring less wood, fewer nails, etc.). These fences, in fact, are some of the fastest of any vertical-board design to erect. After placing the posts and top and bottom rails, you simply mark off the individual board or batten placement with a story stick (a stick 6 feet or longer with markings as reference points). Make sure all boards and battens are the correct length and then start nailing.

Horizontal-board fencing is the fastest to erect for long runs. It usually consists of three or four horizontal boards per panel. You can choose horizontal boards of different widths and place them at different intervals for decoration purposes. Although this fence style is sensible as stock or decorative fencing, it is not effective as security fencing (Illus. 18). The reason is simple: no matter what the spacing, the horizontal boards provide a fairly good ladder for entry into and out of whatever area the fence surrounds. Therefore horizontal-board fences should never be built too close to houses or other structures. In fact, to prevent intrusion, just about any fence that is under 6 feet tall should not be erected close enough to a building so that someone could step or jump from the fence to the structure.

Diagonal-board fence designs (Illus. 19) are a bit more complex than horizontal-fence designs, though the simple X-type fence is most common and is not much harder to construct than a basic three- or four-board fence. If you place two X's in each panel or only part of an X in each panel, then

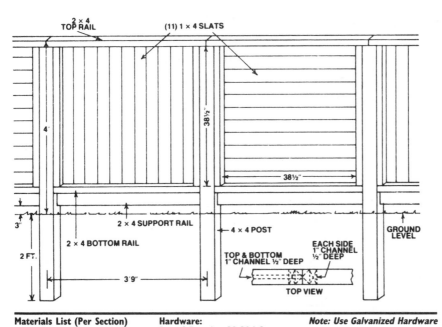

Illus. 18. Alternating horizontal- and vertical-board fence panels.

Diagram labels: 2 × 4 TOP RAIL · (11) 1 × 4 SLATS · 38½" · 4' · 38½" · 3" · 2 × 4 SUPPORT RAIL · 4 × 4 POST · GROUND LEVEL · 2 × 4 BOTTOM RAIL · TOP & BOTTOM 1" CHANNEL ½ DEEP · EACH SIDE 1" CHANNEL ½" DEEP · 2 FT. · 3'9" · TOP VIEW

Materials List (Per Section)
Lumber:
2 Pcs. 4 × 4 × 6' Posts
1 Pc. 2 × 4 × 8' Top Rail
2 Pcs. 2 × 4 × 14' Framing
7 ⅓ Pcs. 1 × 4 × 10'
(Cut 22-3'3½") Slats

Hardware:
2 × 4 Framing 30-20d Common
Nails
1 × 4 Slats 88-6d Common
Nails

For End Section Add:
1 Pc. 4 × 4 × 6' Post

Note: Use Galvanized Hardware

Boards should not be
butted snugly together;
allow space for wood
swelling in humid weather.

Illus. 19. Note the heavy-metal corner bracing on this Construction Common redwood fence. Built as a wind and privacy screen, it needs the extra strength even with diagonally set fence boards and 2″ × 6″ framing that has been set on 6″ × 4″ posts.

construction becomes more complex and consumes more time in measuring and cutting (Illus. 20).

Louvered-board fences (see Illus. 21) are, in one sense, a type of panel

Illus. 20. Such a heavy X-board fence design is generally classified as excellent for equine purposes.

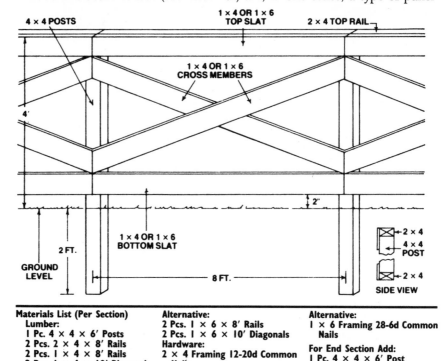

Materials List (Per Section)
Lumber:
 I Pc. 4 × 4 × 6' Posts
 2 Pcs. 2 × 4 × 8' Rails
 2 Pcs. I × 4 × 8' Rails
 2 Pcs. I × 4 × 10' Diagonals

Alternative:
 2 Pcs. I × 6 × 8' Rails
 2 Pcs. I × 6 × 10' Diagonals
Hardware:
 2 × 4 Framing 12-20d Common Nails
 I × 4 Framing 28-6d Common Nails

Alternative:
 I × 6 Framing 28-6d Common Nails

For End Section Add:
 I Pc. 4 × 4 × 6' Post

Note: Use Galvanized Hardware

Illus. 21. A louvered fence.

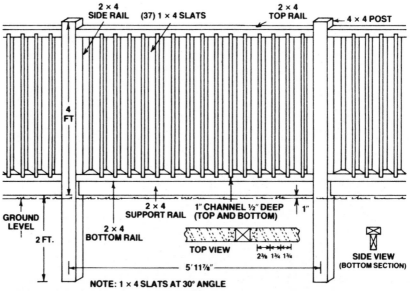

Materials List (Per Section)
Lumber:
 I Pc. 4 × 4 × 6' Post
 3 Pcs. 2 × 4 × 6' Rails
 I Pc. 2 × 4 × 8' (Cut 2–4') Side Supports
 37 Pcs. I × 4 × 3'5½" Slats

Alternative:
 I Pc. I × 4 × 10' (Cut 2–5') Spacers
Hardware:
 2 × 4 Framing 22-20d Common Nails
 I × 4 Framing 148-6d Common Nails

Alternative:
 I × 4 Spacers 152-6d Common Nails
For End Section Add:
 I Pc. 4 × 4 × 6' Post

Note: Use Galvanized Hardware Not recommended for heights over four feet.

Illus. 22. Board fences seldom come much plainer, yet this fence is quite attractive.

fence. It is best to make the louvers vertical and to construct the fence one panel at a time. Then erect each panel between the posts and on top of the bottom rail, should your design require one. Louver fences provide privacy without appearing unneighborly. They are also effective as windbreaks, redirecting the wind instead of trying to totally block it (Illus. 16). Other patterns, such as lattices and basketweaves also make effective windbreaks because they break the force of the wind without creating as much counterpressure as a solid-board fence (Illus. 23, 24).

Illus. 23. Openwork designs are best, whenever possible, for small to moderate size areas.

Illus. 24. This form of open-work fencing does not require the purchase of factory-made, or mill-made, lattice. It is constructed of 2″ × 2″ material, with 4″ × 4″ posts, and 2″ × 6″ and 2″ × 8″ caps. The result is an exceptionally strong screen that is quite easy to make. Simply start the open work as shown, making rectangular panels with two of the shorter 2″ × 2″ members and two of the longer. Attach the longer ones first, using 16d rust-resistant nails, and space them as desired. Normally, the spacing is the same width as the 2″ × 2″s, or 1½ inches. Sheath the posts with 2″ × 6″s, and use 2″ × 8″s to make outside corner turns. The resulting fence provides privacy and protection from the wind and is sturdy, despite its appearance.

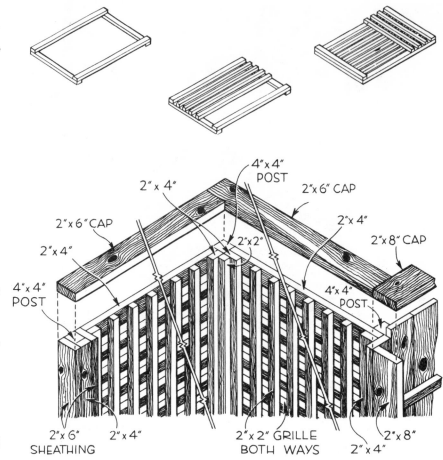

Basic horizontal- or vertical-board fencing is among the most economical of all fencing for the do-it-yourselfer (Illus. 25), though for enclosing small areas they tend to look rather boxy if made of a single design or an uncomplicated but closed pattern. Try alternating patterns or modifying the design slightly on every third or fourth fence panel instead of making every panel identical. If the enclosed area is small, modify the pattern more often (Illus. 26). Using vertical boards to make a windbreak or a privacy fence is great, but the design can seem very boring, especially if the fence is over 6 feet tall. Again, some form of pattern change is needed to break the continuity and add interest. The pattern change—such as attaching an extra board—need not show on the opposite side, but such changes are usually more easily made that way.

Horizontal-board fences of nominal 1-inch lumber are all right if the panels are limited to 10 feet in length but are sturdiest if the limit is 8 feet.

Board fences may also be made with holders, such as those produced by TECO, nailed to the sides of the posts. Slip the board ends into the holders. Then nail the boards through the holders, with the special nails provided, or leave them loose for easy replacement should one rot or break.

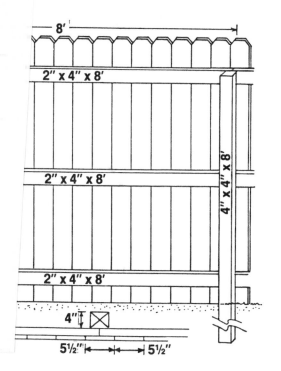

Illus. 25. Plain vertical-board fence design.

8'

2" x 4" x 8'

2" x 4" x 8'

2" x 4" x 8'

4" x 4" x 8'

4"

5½" | 5½"

Materials List
2 Pcs. 4 × 4 × 8' Posts
2 Pcs. 2 × 4 × 8' Braces
18 Pcs. 1 × 6 × 6' Slats

Note: Use Galvanized Hardware

Boards should not be butted snugly together; allow space for wood swelling in humid weather.

Illus. 26. Redwood trellis fence that surrounds a small garden gives some privacy but retains an open feeling.

STOCK FENCING

For extremely heavy stock fencing, erect posts the size of railroad ties and (nominal) 2-inch-thick lumber. In such cases, insert lag screws with washers under the screw head to attach the boards to the posts. Use a lag screw at least two and a half times as long as the board thickness for best results. Only one per board per post is needed then. Again, to increase strength, place boards across two posts before cutting them. The greatest strength is derived from alternating joints over posts. Not many people bother, but if you make two joints (in a three-board fence) on one post, the third joint should be on the preceding or following post. In most cases, a fence this sturdy is built with four boards, which produces symmetrical alternation.

For stock fences, you should nail the boards to the posts on the same side that holds the stock. Strength is much greater then because if the horse, cow, or other animal slams into the fence, the nails won't pop out permitting the animal to escape. If stock is held on both sides of a fence, use a batten over the joints on the post, nailing the batten over the boards that have already been nailed in place. This provides more than a little additional strength.

If you plan to build a board fence for enclosing stock, consider the following. For cattle, board fencing is probably a waste of money except to show off top-grade animals or to provide shuttle pens for loading and unloading vehicles. Barbed wire is as effective and costs far less. For horses, board fencing or board and wire mesh (not chicken-wire mesh, but heavier material, at least 14 gauge in thickness, with moderate size mesh) are close to ideal. The horses can see the fence well, and the fence can be built tall enough to contain the fence hopper of the herd.

Most often, equine fencing problems start when mares come into season and a stallion is pastured nearby. That stallion will try to go over, under, or through just about anything to be near the mare; thus he will need the heaviest equine fencing. Usually, a 5-foot tall board, a post-and-rail, or a wire-and-board fence is sufficient. If the stallion is particularly edgy, you might wish to make it 6 feet. Taller fences are not only expensive to build, they require a great deal more work, and the higher sections are harder to nail. For such temporary needs, you might want to consider simply placing an electric fence about 5 feet on the inside of the pasture where the stallion is. Mark the fence line with rag strips or old pie plates and turn the power on. This electric fence "liner" should be placed about 3 feet high, and the current should always be on.

Except for the expense of lightweight metal or fibreglass poles (one of which is needed about every 20 feet with electric fencing), the installation costs, including charger, wire, and gate handle and insulators, are very reasonable. If your pasture is exceptionally large, the total cost should never be more than one third more, including fibreglass posts (which I prefer, simply because they're easy to insert and don't require insulators, which further reduce costs).

Making shallow notches in the poles can facilitate the attachment of heavy boards at times. In some fences, like the one in Illus. 27 with alternating panels, the windbreak effect is very good. Note that the vertical boards, though, have been improperly nailed: nails not protected with galvanizing material have been used, so there are rust streaks on the wood. Note also that the wood was chosen from a grade that allows loose knots, some of which have fallen out, adding visual interest to the fence.

Illus. 27. In this vertical-board fence with panels that alternate sides, you can see the clinched nails on the rails, as well as rust streaks from the mild steel, uncoated nails.

FOUND-MATERIAL FENCES

The fence in Illus. 28 was made with found materials, in this case shipping pallets. Pallets are readily available from many printing and shipping companies. I use them for fast-burning wood fires and kindling during the winter, but as the illustration shows, they also make good fences. This fence is in Arizona. The pallets have been tied together with heavy wire and attached to corner posts of lightweight wood. There are very few intermediate posts, and yet the fence is strong enough to contain sheep or cattle exceptionally well. It won't, however, serve as well for hogs, which root under a fence to get out to something seemingly more attractive. It should be moderately effective for containing gentle horses, depending on the height of the pallets. As a decorative fence, however, it totally fails, of course.

Illus. 28. Pallets make a sturdy and inexpensive fence.

Another fence of found materials is shown in Illus. 29, this time old wagon wheels are the major component. Note how the boards have been designed and attached to hold the wagon wheels with moderate security. A block has been placed under each wheel to hold it at the correct height. Even the gate is comprised of a wagon wheel. This sort of fence is quite decorative and says something about the owner, I think. First, the owner must be fairly persistent to have located and stored so many wagon wheels. Second, his design is interesting and unique. Note on the gate how the heavy spring is set so it pulls the gate shut, using a chain through the hub of the wheel. The gate opens inward, away from the spring, making its placement just about perfect.

Illus. 29. This wagon wheel fence is an excellent example of using materials on hand, or easily located, to make an unusual and attractive design.

Further use of found materials is shown in Illus. 30 where the middle of some cable reels have been removed, the tops and bottoms cut in half, and the sections used as a decorative background to a metal-post barbed-wire fence. You could call this either a wire fence or a board fence, I guess, but in

Illus. 30. Halves of cable-reel tops and bottoms are used to dress up an otherwise dreary wire fence.

any case its unusual inclusion of boards presents a very interesting solution to the unrelenting lines of barbed-wire fencing.

All in all, it is possible to construct board fences in so many ways that no two need to be alike unless you wish them to be so.

By following the general construction procedures in Chapter 10, you will provide the necessary strength for any board or panel fence. Panel fencing, though, becomes somewhat more complex because the units are bigger and are often solid or nearly so (Illus. 31a–e), presenting a broad face to the wind and weather. Getting the fence to stay up in high winds can be a problem, then. In fact, some places have such high winds that even latticework fences fall down and eventually must be replaced with openwork brick walls.

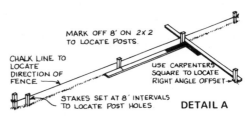

MARK OFF 8' ON 2×2 TO LOCATE POSTS.
CHALK LINE TO LOCATE DIRECTION OF FENCE.
USE CARPENTERS SQUARE TO LOCATE RIGHT ANGLE OFFSET.
STAKES SET AT 8' INTERVALS TO LOCATE POST HOLES.

DETAIL A

Illus. 31a–e. Screen fence design details.

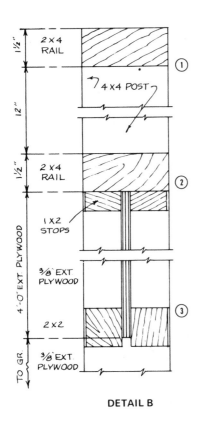

DETAIL B

1. *Locate the fence and post positions as shown in Detail A. Posts should be made of redwood or cedar, although other material may be used if treated or impregnated with wood preservative to ensure durability in the ground. Position each post, using level or plumb bob to set to true vertical. Tamp dirt to pack tightly or set in concrete.*

2. *Trim plywood panels to length and edge seal them with a thick lead and oil paint or other suitable compound. With 4d nails, nail the 2 × 2's horizontally on each side of the bottom of the panel, slightly recessing the panel as shown on Detail B-3. Then cut four side stops to fit between batten and the top of the panel.*

MATERIALS LIST

Recommended plywood:
APA grade-trademarked A-C Exterior, Medium Density Overlay (MDO) or any of the 303 textured plywood sidings

PLYWOOD

Quantity	Description
4 panels	3/8 in. × 4 ft × 8 ft plywood

OTHER MATERIALS

Quantity	Description
48 lin. ft	4 × 4 posts, preferably redwood or cedar
As required	Creosote or other preservative for treating below-ground portion of posts
68 lin. ft	2 × 4 for open upper rails
128 lin. ft	2 × 2 for bottom and center supports
152 lin. ft	1 × 2 for stops
1/2 lb approx.	16d galvanized common (or box) nails for nailing rails to posts
2-1/2 lb approx.	8d galvanized common (or box) nails for fastening 2 × 2's and assembling rails
3/4 lb approx.	4d galvanized nails for installing stops
As required	Paint or stain for finishing, including edge sealer

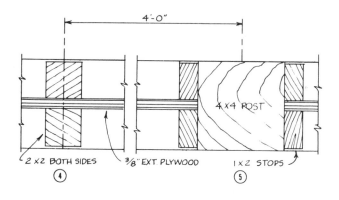

4'-0"

2 X 2 BOTH SIDES

④

3/8" EXT PLYWOOD

4 X 4 POST

1 X 2 STOPS

⑤

DETAIL B

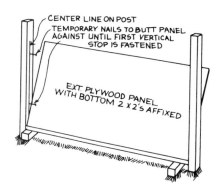

CENTER LINE ON POST
TEMPORARY NAILS TO BUTT PANEL
AGAINST UNTIL FIRST VERTICAL
STOP IS FASTENED

EXT. PLYWOOD PANEL
WITH BOTTOM 2 X 2's AFFIXED

DETAIL C

3. Mark a center line on the inside of each post to locate plywood panel in vertical position. Set the exterior plywood panel on blocks which raise it about 4 inches from the ground, positioning it between the posts. Hold panel in place vertically by setting temporary nails in the posts, on one side of the panel (Detail C). Then nail one stop to each post as shown on Detail B-5. Fasten panel to stops. Remove temporary nails from other side of panel and fasten stops on that side.

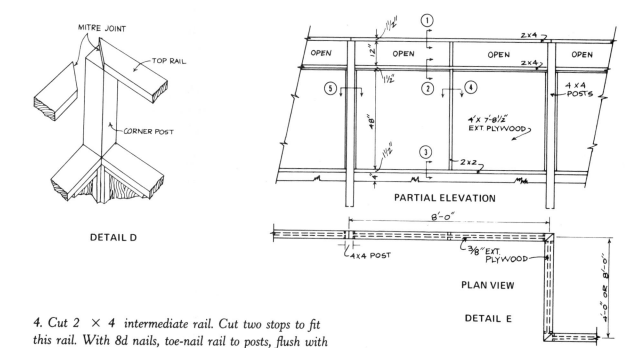

MITRE JOINT

TOP RAIL

CORNER POST

DETAIL D

PARTIAL ELEVATION

OPEN   OPEN   OPEN   OPEN

2 X 4

2 X 4

4 X 4 POSTS

4' X 7'-8½"
EXT. PLYWOOD

2 X 2

12"

1½"

1½"

4'-8"

1½"

4"

① ② ④ ③ ⑤

8'-0"

4 X 4 POST

3/8" EXT.
PLYWOOD

PLAN VIEW

DETAIL E

4'-0" OR 8'-0"

4. Cut 2 × 4 intermediate rail. Cut two stops to fit this rail. With 8d nails, toe-nail rail to posts, flush with the top of the panel. Then nail the two stops in place as shown in B-2.

In general, solid or nearly solid panel fences require posts of the same size as regular board fencing: line posts should be 4″ × 4″, while corner and gate posts must be at least 6″ × 6″. If you design a fence with boards on both sides, you may wish to use 2″ × 4″ line posts, but in such cases the distance between post centers should never be more than 6 feet. If your panel fence is likely to be hit with high winds, use 6″ × 6″ line posts and 8″ × 8″ corner and gate posts. For erecting standard board fences, the rule of thumb is one-third of a fence post should be inserted into the ground. You can even insert less on longer posts for a higher fence if stresses won't be high. But for panel fences, you *must* have one-third of the post in the ground, and two-fifths or more is better.

Illus. 32. Finished drawing of the stepped screen fence

© 1976 American Plywood Association

For most panel fencing, you have a wide, wide choice not only of materials but of construction methods. Most will be on 4-foot centers for maximum rigidity, but beyond that, you can install posts, place upper and lower rails, and then nail panels of whatever material you choose to the rails. Or you can install the posts and build the panels on the ground, including all rails and panel braces. With a helper, you then install the finished panel on the standing posts. Postholes may be dug, the posts laid out on the ground, and the panels built onto them, after which the section(s) may be tipped into the holes, plumbed, and the holes filled.

The designs for panel fences are so numerous that it would be impossible to cover them all. Your choice depends on your particular containment needs and your imagination. My recommendations are simple: keep solid or near solid panel-fencing sections as short as possible, changing to board, wire or post-and-rail fencing as soon as practical when covering a greater length. Use nails at least three times as long as the material being nailed. In other words, if you're nailing into 1-inch material, use 3-inch (10 penny, or 10d) nails. If nails penetrate the materials, clinch the ends to add strength. Use only hot-dipped galvanized nails or aluminum nails. Lag screws or carriage bolts must also be galvanized (Illus. 33). If the wood above ground

Illus. 33. With railroad ties as posts and lag screws as fasteners for the boards, this cattle chute fence is plenty sturdy.

is not pressure treated or naturally resistant, coat it carefully before construction (but after cutting to size) with a suitable preservative. To paint the fence, lay on the prime coat before it's erected so that the interior of the joints will be coated for greater durability. Use a spray gun to apply the next coat. I suggest an airless spray gun because it has less of an overspray problem than the other types. The surrounding area, therefore, will not be the same color as the fence during its first year.

Following such methods, you should be able to build board or panel fences with relative ease, and they should last as long as the posts in the ground last, which could be 100 years. If unprotected materials are used as rails, boards, or in panels, expect to have some weathering problems within a decade if the fence is not treated with preservative or coated with paint every three years or so (Illus. 34, 35).

Illus. 34. Channel panel fence. A groove has been formed in the top and bottom rails.

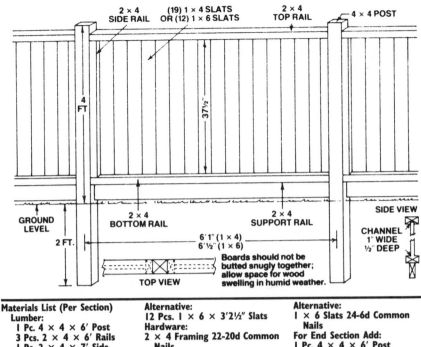

2 × 4 SIDE RAIL
(19) 1 × 4 SLATS OR (12) 1 × 6 SLATS
2 × 4 TOP RAIL
4 × 4 POST
4 FT
37½"
GROUND LEVEL
2 FT.
2 × 4 BOTTOM RAIL
2 × 4 SUPPORT RAIL
SIDE VIEW
CHANNEL 1" WIDE ½" DEEP
6' 1" (1 × 4)
6' ½" (1 × 6)
Boards should not be butted snugly together; allow space for wood swelling in humid weather.
TOP VIEW

Materials List (Per Section)
Lumber:
  1 Pc. 4 × 4 × 6' Post
  3 Pcs. 2 × 4 × 6' Rails
  1 Pc. 2 × 4 × 7' Side Supports
  19 Pcs. 1 × 4 × 3'2½" Slats

Alternative:
  12 Pcs. 1 × 6 × 3'2½" Slats
Hardware:
  2 × 4 Framing 22-20d Common Nails
  1 × 4 Framing 38-6d Common Nails

Alternative:
  1 × 6 Slats 24-6d Common Nails
For End Section Add:
  1 Pc. 4 × 4 × 6' Post

Note: Use Galvanized Hardware

Illus. 35. Alternating panels of two different width boards can add a great deal of interest to a fence.

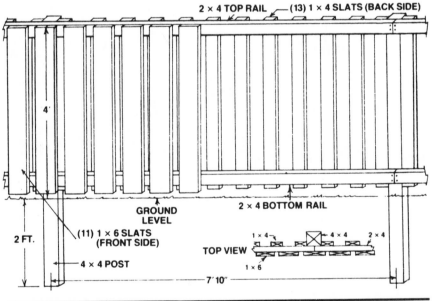

2 × 4 TOP RAIL
(13) 1 × 4 SLATS (BACK SIDE)
4'
GROUND LEVEL
2 × 4 BOTTOM RAIL
2 FT.
(11) 1 × 6 SLATS (FRONT SIDE)
4 × 4 POST
TOP VIEW
1 × 4
4 × 4
2 × 4
1 × 6
7' 10"

Materials List (Per Section)
Lumber:
  1 Pc. 4 × 4 × 6' Post
  2 Pcs. 2 × 4 × 8' Rails
  13 Pcs. 1 × 4 × 3'11" Slats
  11 Pcs. 1 × 6 × 1'11" Slats

Hardware:
  2 × 4 Framing 24-20d Common Nails
  1 × 4 & 1 × 6 Framing 96-6d Common Nails

For End Section Add:
  1 Pc. 4 × 4 × 6' Post
  1 Pc. 1 × 4 × 3'11" Slat

Note: Use Galvanized Hardware For slats longer than four feet, add an intermediate rail for greater support.

3 · Picket Fences

Most people envision a residential fence as a picket fence that surrounds a small cottage, sometimes with a Tom Sawyer-like character slapping on whitewash with an oversize brush. The everyday picket fence has been the most popular town fence for many years and will retain its position for years to come for several reasons (Illus. 37 on page 38).

First, the cost of materials is relatively low because the fence is seldom over 3 feet tall. Second, it is virtually always attractive even if erected badly. Third, there are probably 500 or more variations on the original design (Illus. 36), including a shaped-end fence (Illus. 38) of horizontal pickets.

Illus. 36. A contemporary good-neighbor fence of economical knot-textured Construction Heart redwood invites comfortable, private, outdoor living and is attractive from both sides. The buckskin tan color can be stabilized by applying a clear water repellent. Redwood takes and holds finishes better than other woods because of its open cellular structure.

Picket fences are, in essence, post-and-rail fences with widely spaced rails. The spaces are filled in with pickets. The classic picket fence may have posts at 6-foot intervals and rails spaced as required for the fence height.

Illus. 37. This is what some people call a classic picket fence.

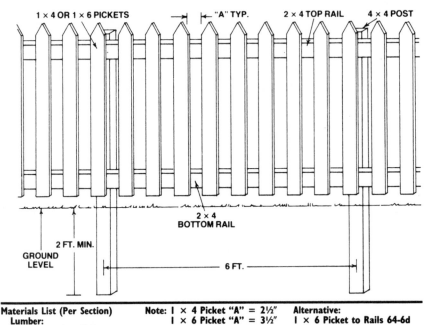

Materials List (Per Section)
Lumber:
  1 Pc. 4 × 4 × 8' Post
  2 Pcs. 2 × 4 × 6' Rails
  12 Pcs. 1 × 4 × 5' Pickets
Alternate:
  8 Pcs. 1 × 6 × 5' Pickets

Note: 1 × 4 Picket "A" = 2½"
      1 × 6 Picket "A" = 3½"
Hardware:
  Rails to Posts 8-20d
    Common Nails
  Picket to Rails 96-6d
    Common Nails

Alternative:
  1 × 6 Picket to Rails 64-6d
    Common Nails
For End Section:
  1 Post, 1 Picket
  8-6d Common Nails

Illus. 38. A horizontal (shaped-end) picket fence is a bit more unusual than the ordinary vertical fence.

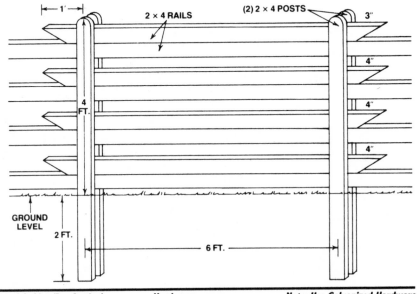

Materials List (Per Section)
Lumber:
  4 Pcs. 2 × 4 × 6' Posts
  4 Pcs. 2 × 4 × 12' Rails
  4 Pcs. 2 × 4 × 8' Rails
    w/Shaped Ends

Hardware:
Post to Rails 80-10d
  Common Nails

For Section Add:
  2 Pcs. 2 × 4 × 6' Posts
  48-10d Common Nails

Note: Use Galvanized Hardware

Pickets may be cut at the classic 45° angle on the top, or cut with a convex curve instead of a straight line. Or you may desire to make palings, a form of picket in which one side is sloped at a 45° or 60° angle. Such fences, when higher than the normal 3- to 3½-foot picket fence, tend to be hazardous for anyone trying to climb over them.

For decorative pickets, there's almost no limit to the designs you might choose from (Illus. 39). You may wish to use a hole saw to cut a design through the picket after the board has been cut at its top and bottom. Use a jigsaw to cut fanciful and curved picket tops.

In general, pickets should measure 1″ × 4″ or 1″ × 6″ to form a sturdy fence. For light and low fences, 1″ × 3″ material is fine. Posts should be made of 4″ × 4″ pressure-treated or naturally resistant wood, while bottom and top rails should match the posts. Such construction ensures a sturdy fence when rails are attached to posts with 16d nails and when the pickets are attached with 6d or 8d nails. Use two nails for 4-inch-wide pickets and three nails for wider ones (Illus. 40).

Pickets don't have to have pointed tops. In fact, if children play in the neighborhood, choose some form of round-top design. It can look just as

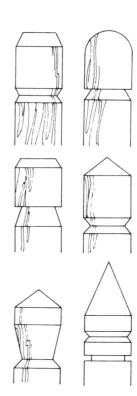

Illus. 39. Here are some basic picket-top designs.

Illus. 40. Note how the heavy end and corner posts are formed on this redwood picket fence. Consider the need for such bracing when planning your own fence.

good and can also prevent lawsuits. Flat-top pickets may also work well as may a number of other designs. You can buy precut pickets at lumberyards and building supply stores, though to me this takes a great deal of the fun out of putting up this form of fence. It is simpler, though more costly, when you don't have the proper tools to make the cuts.

Essentially, your tool requirements for forming pickets include a jigsaw and a belt sander. The Skil belt sander in Illus. 41 is designed to be operated upside down, with clamps holding it in place. It can be used to finish already-cut pickets or to form pickets that don't have many curves. Just by rotating a flat picket end against an 80-grit belt you will take off enough material at the corners of the picket to produce a nicely rounded style.

Illus. 41. Skil's Sand Hawg is designed to be used upside down, as shown, but clamps are needed to make sure it doesn't wander from designated points.

In order to make all pickets in the same style and length, make a cardboard template of your design. There are many typical picket fence designs to choose from (See Illus. 39.) Look for one that pleases you and suits the architecture of your home. First, trace the design and then enlarge or reduce it as necessary. Be sure your width measurement is correct and then fold the template in half. Cut out half of the design on one side of the picket. Then unfold the template: the sides are now cut identically.

In addition, place the pickets close enough together to prevent small children from sticking their heads through the slats. If you erect 4-inch pickets, place them 3 inches apart. If the distance is greater, use alternate pickets, that is, use one picket on the inside of the fence and one on the outside.

Picket fences provide only minimal protection against intruders because they are generally too low and too weak. But they are useful for containing small animals of many types and for keeping small children within sight.

If you think that the picket fence is a cliché, look for ways to either vary your design or else erect another kind of fence. You could, for instance, place four pickets on one side of the rails and four on the other, or vary the widths of the pickets to improve the fence's appearance. Different height pickets or horizontal pickets might also be attractive.

All in all, it's pretty much up to the builder. If you like a design, then use it. If you don't like it, don't use it. If consulted on the fence's design, your neighbor should carry only so much influence, since the final decision is, of course, up to you.

Remember, too, that various designs of picket fences are available in partially assembled units at certain lumberyards. This can save you a lot of time, though it will cost more money. All you do is dig the postholes and tip the fence into place, making sure all is lined up and plumb. Be sure your measurements are accurate here, for there's far less leeway with manufactured fences than with those you build yourself.

In your own construction, erect posts made of pressure-treated or naturally resistant wood that is meant to be used in ground. Slats and rails can be made of less well treated wood. The amount of preservative retained in pressure-treated lumber has a strong bearing on the price of that lumber, so don't waste money getting everything treated for in-ground use if some of it is to be used above ground. Insert only aluminum or galvanized nails or screws for fasteners (or brass screws).

The resulting fence should be quite pleasing to most everyone.

Illus. 42. Shaped Construction Heart redwood pickets are exceptionally attractive.

4 • Post-and-Rail Fences

Of all simple fences, the rail and post-and-rail fences are always extremely popular. They require no nailing and little carpentry, while the factory-produced units require little more than a fairly accurate posthole-to-posthole measurement, some digging, and simply tipping the post into place.

Homemade post-and-rail fences, especially the split-rail type, are more laborious but require only a few tools for construction, which has added to their popularity over the years. An axe (not essential, but helpful), a splitting maul, two or three splitting wedges, and a posthole digger are all you need. And, in fact, you can use the axe to build your own maul of wood, and the wedges can also be of wood, instead of the steel ones used these days.

If you have no posthole digger and no shovel, rail-on-rail fences can be constructed quite easily. These zigzag, or "snake," fences stand for years and years, depending on the wood used. The bottom rail of every other unit comes in direct contact with the ground, so it is rather quickly subject to rot in certain areas. Woods such as cedar and chestnut prevent rot for a long, long time, and the keepers of the Blue Ridge Parkway (Illus. 1) have stored enough chestnut rails to last from fifty to one hundred more years; it's quite possible that by that time someone will have figured out a cure for the blight that is killing adult chestnuts. Because the chestnut generates its own shoots from stumps, if the blight is cured or otherwise held back, we will again have examples of this majestic and useful tree.

Most people today erect zigzag fences of cedar. It's easy to find and easy to split, and is very, very attractive once it weathers a while (six to eighteen or twenty-four months).

Another form of homemade rail fence includes a double post, through which rails are laid alternately, as shown in Illus. 43. The main problem with this style of fence is that like the snake fence, it requires a large amount

Illus. 43. Double-post and rail fence.

of material. In addition, you must dig postholes. Be sure to use a durable wood, like cedar, for the posts and for at the very least every other bottom rail since they will be resting directly on the ground. I suggest using cedar for all the rails for a simple reason: it is not expensive and is often free for the cutting in many areas because of apple-cedar rust (a blight that just looks bad on cedars but kills apple trees). Even if you must buy cedar, it should not be expensive since the form needed here is rough cut and unfinished, and often the sizes available won't even require splitting.

Wire the double posts together at the tops using thick (about 12- to 10-gauge) aluminum wire, after laying the rails. Fence height is a function of your needs and desires. You can save more money here if you can find small enough cedar that needs no splitting. The entire fence may be built with nothing more than a shovel, a saw (or axe), and a pair of fencing pliers (to cut and twist the aluminum wire). If you make the postholes large enough to hold two posts at once, with enough room (about 6 to 8 inches) between to hold a small rock that will keep them separated, you don't even need a posthole digger.

READY-MADE POST-AND-RAIL FENCES

Ready-made posts and rails differ markedly from homemade versions (Illus. 44). They are somewhat neater looking and virtually all are pressure-

treated, which turns them a light shade of green. Some pressure-treated woods are made with nearly colorless chemicals, and a few are manufactured with a brown color. If left to weather normally, however, in six months to a year almost all woods begin to turn grey.

Designing a post-and-rail fence is similar to designing a board or other type of fence. If you want to contain stallions, erect the fence so that there is at least 5 feet between the top rail and the ground (with three rails) and preferably 6 feet of height (with four rails). If colts are in the field, the lower rail must be no less than 12 inches above the ground, and no farther than 18 inches (those little animals can squirm when they get curious).

Two-rail fences (Illus. 45) are best for decorative purposes, for holding milk cows, or for a few (under a dozen) beef cattle in a large pasture. They are not suitable for much else.

As mentioned in Chapter 10 (page 94) you should set end posts firmly, but set intermediate or line posts loosely until you have placed all the rails in a row. It's simply a matter of wiggle to fit, and if the posts are set solid, you can't wiggle and nothing fits.

In general, post-and-rail fences are far more popular than my short treatment of them here seems to indicate. In fact, in many areas of the East, they are about the most popular style of fencing. The reasons are many. They are fairly inexpensive to build, they can be designed in a number of styles, and you could erect at least small sections with wood from your own property. In addition, post-and-rail fences vary widely in their applications:

Illus. 45. The square rails are supported with blocks, making this a sturdy and attractive fence.

a decorative two-rail fence, although very attractive and somewhat useful, is far, far different from a tall, sturdy four-rail fence.

Factory-produced panels of rail fencing are easy to erect. Seldom are the panels less than 10 feet wide, while some with thicker rails may be 12 feet wide, so the number of postholes you must dig is much smaller than you would need for a louver, vertical-board, or picket fence.

While the post-and-rail fence looks fine with a rustic-style house, it also complements many contemporary designs. Post-and-rail fencing, then, goes equally well around a gambrel-roofed New England Colonial house, a California "adobe" rancho, or an East Coast brick ranch-style house.

Whether you choose the Abe Lincoln style or the modern factory-produced mortise-and-tenon style, be assured that the popularity of the post-and-rail fence will be just as high in several decades as it is now.

5 • Stock and Pet Fences

Providing fencing for stock or pets can vary greatly depending on whether you wish to protect the humans from animals or vice versa.

For small dogs, a picket fence or a relatively low (4-feet-tall) chain-link fence is generally considered sufficient to keep them out of trouble. By the same token, small children should be reasonably well protected by the same types of construction. Though, honestly, I shudder at the thought of any child of mine playing unsupervised in a yard protected only by a fence. I'd want someone watching at all times. For children, use a slightly more complex gate latch to prevent them from slipping out.

For cats, you will have to design a special enclosure. I've never seen the fence our cats couldn't climb should the desire arise, and ours are well fed and lazy. A fence with a top is the only answer for them.

STOCK FENCING

Stock fences must vary with the type of stock, though not in the basic construction as much as one might think. Cattle may be held in wooden pens, though in practice barbed wire is used much more frequently.

With the exception of an angry bull or cow, cattle are more phlegmatic, less excitable, than horses. Thus you need only a fairly strong fence that will let them know it's there when they brush against it, more than anything else. Barbed wire does a superb job of that, and many modern types don't make massive slashes into the animals that some of the older brands do (Illus. 46).

Effective pig fences are difficult to design. Adult pigs aren't so destructive, except when they hit one fence section they tend to pack an awful lot of weight in a very low slung area over and over again, bumping the fence down low, where rot and other structural weaknesses tend to appear first. And, of course, they love to scratch. Piglets are a real annoyance because

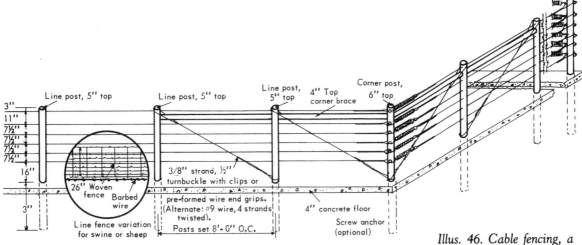

Line post, 5" top   Line post, 5" top   Line post, 5" top   4" Top corner brace   Corner post, 6" top

3"
11"
7½"
7½"
7½"
7½"
16"

26" Woven fence   Barbed wire

3"

Line fence variation for swine or sheep

3/8" strand, ½" turnbuckle with clips or pre-formed wire end grips. (Alternate: #9 wire, 4 strands twisted).

Posts set 8'-0" O.C.

4" concrete floor

Screw anchor (optional)

Illus. 46. Cable fencing, a form of wire fencing, may be varied to suit many animals.

they seem capable of slipping through a pinhole and heading for the nearest expensively sodded pasture or lawn, where they'll happily grub away for hours (literally looking for grubworms), while reducing several thousand dollars worth of Mrs. Pennypacker's lawn to a 7-pence shambles. This does not add to your list of friends, though it will likely add to your list of legal acquaintances.

For adult pigs, erect fence boards of 2-inch pressure-treated southern pine, with 6″ × 6″ posts. To contain piglets, run one electric fence line 2 to 3 inches above ground level and a second one 4 to 6 inches above ground level, just inside the main fence. This is only a temporary measure, which is fortunate because every animal will be unhappy with it, and an unhappy pig is almost as noisy as an unhappy politician. Once the piglets reach a size about double that of a regulation football, shut the current off for a few days and see what happens. If the piglets remain inside the fence, then you can remove it.

Stock fencing in general has a lot to do with the desired condition of hides, as well as with the overall health of the animals. If you don't mind a few scars here and there, you can use barbed wire. If a glistening and pure hide is essential, you need to install a board or heavy wire mesh fence. A great deal varies, as well, from area to area.

As far as sheep go, I've seen them in rock pens, wooden pens, wire-mesh pens, and barbed-wire pens. If nothing frightens them, there's never a problem. Unfortunately, sheep frighten easily, and if there are many in the group, there's a problem no matter what kind of fence surrounds them. Sheep pile up when frightened instead of fleeing as do most other animals. That is, if there's a corner big enough for three sheep to feel safe in, and there are sixty frightened sheep in the pen, there will be anywhere from forty-nine to sixty frightened sheep piled in that corner, with the predictable results for those on the bottom.

Large fields or small groups seem to me to be the only solution to keeping sheep safe, regardless of the type of fence used.

HORSE FENCING

Fencing for horses ranges from the least to the most complex. Horses require a sturdy fence that is easy to see and is made of a material that won't break into spearlike splinters when the fence is struck hard. For temporary,

Illus. 47. Post-and-board joint. This is not a good design, because no matter how well you attach it, the top board can be knocked loose too easily.

general purposes for geldings and mares past the fractious age, use single-or double-wire electric fencing. The cost is very reasonable. For stallions, particularly those held near brood mares, fencing must be of a much different sort, though it may well include an inner double-wire electric fence to at least slow down the animal before it arrives at the outer fence. Horses can clear incredible heights when properly motivated and if they aren't carrying a rider. Most of us cannot even think of building fences tall enough to hold a stallion in pursuit of a mare, but the shock from an electric fence that is placed 6 to 8 feet or so inside a 5-foot-tall board, or a four-rail post-and-rail fence, will force the horse to break his stride as he prepares to leap the outer fence.

For general equine fencing, three-board fences at least 42 inches high are sufficient. For slightly better security with Arabians and Thoroughbreds, consider a fence 48 to 60 inches high as a standard, with 72-inch-high fencing for Thoroughbred stallions. Arabian horses do not normally need such tall fencing for several reasons: they're generally smaller horses, which limits their jumping capabilities somewhat, and they are also seemingly friendlier towards people, less skittish, and more playful.

The more active the horse, the higher the fence, at least until full-time boundaries are determined. Geldings can often be left inside an electric fence for 5 to 6 weeks with the current on. After that you need turn the current on only intermittently as a reminder.

Fence construction and materials are of equal, or greater, importance than fence height. An escaped horse may not be as unfortunate as one that runs into a white-oak board fence, breaking a board and getting speared. Use pine, not oak, for wooden fences for horses. Redwood is neither strong enough for large, active horses, nor is it inexpensive enough for a large area. For smaller areas, such as paddocks where four- and five-board fences are common, it is ideal. Barbed wire is used too often to contain horses. It's not until you have to treat a foot-long wound or shoot a horse because the wounds are too bad to treat that the danger is impressed on you.

Eastern Thoroughbreds that would tear themselves to ribbons if caught in barbed wire fences must have board fence, or at the least board and wire mesh fencing. Western-range-bred horses, however, are colder blooded and more likely to stand steady once caught in something, instead of thrashing about in panic. So, fortunately, the need to use barbed wire on large cattle ranches poses less of a danger to these horses.

Wire-mesh fencing is less expensive than continuous-board fencing when a lot of pasture needs to be enclosed. In such cases, though, the mesh should be 4 inches square or smaller, and the fence should have a board at least 6 inches wide at the top to improve visibility.

Be sure to place the lowest board of a board fence at least 12 inches from the ground. For wire fences attach a similar board bottom or a smaller wire mesh (3 inches square) no closer than 12 to 18 inches from the ground. Horses require at least this much space under a fence so that in case they lie or fall their foot doesn't get caught under a fence board or any other obstacle (including some stall interior boards). If it does happen, the horse is cast and will often break a leg thrashing around to get free. The hoof *must* be capable of being drawn free by a panicked animal.

Actually, equine fencing is a simple matter if one keeps in mind the horse's tendency to panic easily and its great size. After all, even small horses can weigh as much as 650 pounds when grown.

There are, of course, dozens of other forms of stock and pet fencing, but some we can't cover because they're too specialized. And many types of fences can be used for two different kinds of animals: cows and sheep do quite well in similarly fenced surroundings, in most cases, for example, and any horse fence will suit cattle (though all cattle fences will not suit horses).

Illus. 48. Three fences suitable for stock.

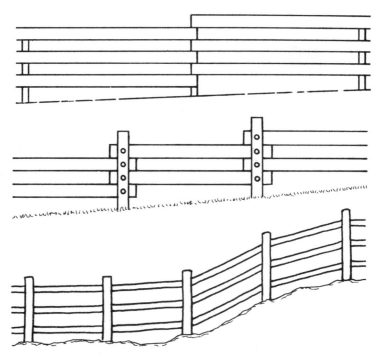

Any fencing not covered here for stock and pets is not because I don't think they're worthwhile. Most stock fencing is adaptable from one breed or species to another, and the same holds true with fencing for pets (Illus. 48, 49). Unless you decide to get an exotic pet or to collect cheetahs, the fences included here should do the job. If you do choose to contain an exotic animal, be sure to check first the laws about keeping such animals confined, with or without permits, and also be sure you can care for the animals on a long-term basis so they benefit instead of suffer from the experience.

50

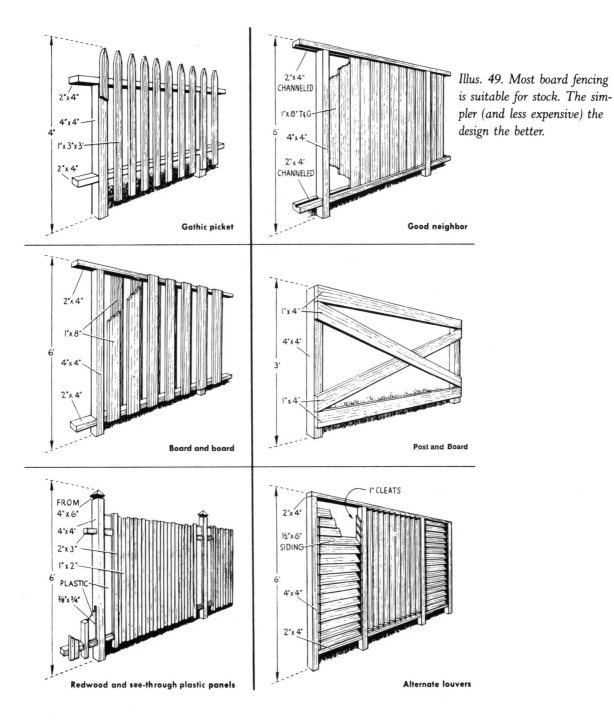

Illus. 49. Most board fencing is suitable for stock. The simpler (and less expensive) the design the better.

Gothic picket

2"x 4"
4"x 4"
1"x 3"x 3'
2"x 4"
4'
4"

Good neighbor

2"x 4" CHANNELED
1"x 8" T&G
4"x 4"
2"x 4" CHANNELED
6'

Board and board

2"x 4"
1"x 8"
4"x 4"
2"x 4"
6'

Post and Board

1"x 4"
4"x 4"
1"x 4"
3'

Redwood and see-through plastic panels

FROM 4"x 6"
4"x 4"
2"x 3"
1"x 2"
PLASTIC
3/8"x 3/4"
6'

Alternate louvers

1" CLEATS
2"x 4"
1/2"x 6" SIDING
4"x 4"
2"x 4"
6'

6 · Wire Fences

CHAIN-LINK FENCES

While chain-link fences tend to be thought of as industrial looking, they do serve better than almost any other type as security fences around swimming pools and yards where there are small children or pets (Illus. 50). They're also among the most expensive fences. Be sure to make a detailed design so you will know exactly how much material you will need to do the job. Of the many patterns, the diamond-mesh chain-link material is one of the most difficult to install.

Most styles are galvanized, but it is a simple matter today to get chain-link fencing coated with colored vinyl which serves better than paint to prevent rust and also provides a less factory-looking finish.

Illus. 50. This chain-link fence provides good security while retaining visibility within the secured area.

As with all fences, once you have roughly determined the area to be enclosed and checked the codes, you stake out the fence line. (See Chapter 9, page 88.) Installation of a chain-link fence then requires only six steps for the do-it-yourselfer: (1) setting the end, or termination, posts; (2) setting the intermediate posts; (3) adding any fittings to the posts, as necessary; (4) adding the top rail; (5) hanging the chain-link fabric; and (6) stretching the fabric.

Obviously this omits such necessary items as posthole digging and gate hanging, but those are common to the installation of all fences and are considered a part of the post-setting steps and general techniques described in Chapter 10, page 94.

OTHER WIRE FENCES

Other forms of wire fencing abound. Most require solid posts of light-weight wood with built-in hooks, but many use the basic round, wooden post, with wires that have been attached with staples (Illus. 51, 52). Electric fences and barbed-wire fences are, of course, two forms of wire fences.

Illus. 51 (left). Western barbed-wire fence.

Illus. 52 (right). Corner and gate posts for wire fences must always be braced.

These fences may be erected with virtually any style of post you wish, though electric fences require insulators on all but fibreglass posts (Illus. 53, 54).

In addition to chain-link fences, mesh fences are also widely available. Hexagonal chicken-wire mesh on driven metal posts is used often for

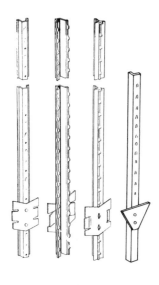

Illus. 53. Common steel-posts models.

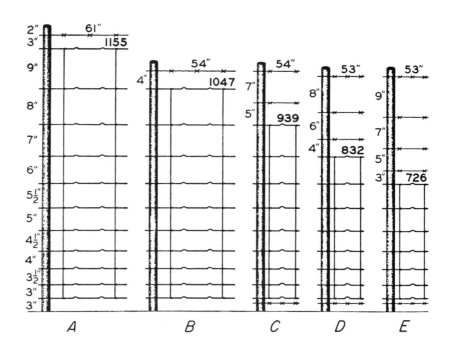

Illus. 54. Woven-wire designs.

garden fencing (Illus. 55). It is lightweight but is very effective unless your area abounds in digging or jumping animals. Digging animals are generally easier to outwit: simply bury about a foot of the fencing in a trench along the entire line. Deer that wish to taste your newly ripening corn are another matter. It's not easy to build a fence high enough to keep a determined deer either in or out. What they can't jump, they can often climb. I suggest making such a fence no higher than 6 feet. (Any taller than that and you'd be spending so much money for the fence that buying vegetables would be cheaper.) Planting a separate plot of the deer's favorite corn *outside* the fence might be another solution. After all, a pound or two of corn seed isn't that expensive.

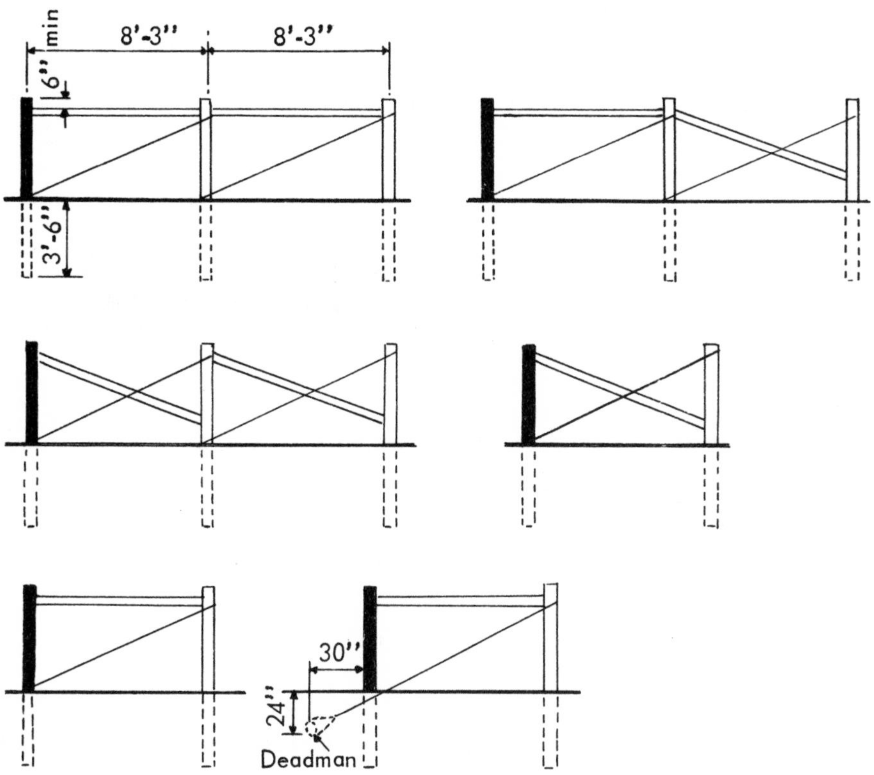

Illus. 55. Bracing methods for different spots along a wire fence.

Garden fences are seldom fancy and seldom need to be. There's usually too much daytime activity for a prowler, so simply keeping rabbits, raccoons, and other small animals out at night suffices. Using the cheapest wire-mesh materials and the cheapest posts is usually best, especially when you're just starting a garden. As time passes, you may want to enlarge the garden because you find that your family consumes a lot more vegetables when they come directly from your own field. Or you may want to move it from an area where the plants pick up diseases or to a slightly more fertile area.

Thus, with a garden fence, if you start with the least expensive materials, expanding later will be less costly.

7 ✦ Fence Materials

When shopping for fencing materials, look for bargains, which could mean a savings of many, many dollars in the overall job. And purchasing the correct materials will not only save you money now, but will mean that the fence will still be standing and doing its job for many years in the future.

WOODS

There is some dispute over the durability of a few wood species when they come in contact with the ground. One such species is post, or black, locust. I believe that it, like white oak, does not last a great deal longer than ten years, and I have been taken to task by some of my neighbors in the rural South who claim locust has an in-ground life of at least twenty years. Well, there's no way to decide, short of testing. If you live in an area where locust grows, however, you will find that it is an exceptionally cheap wood to use for almost any kind of fence. And it is a significantly popular enough wood that the price per post increases dramatically once you go beyond its growing range (150 or so miles).

In general, only very few untreated woods that are normally used in carpentry are suitable for fences. Exceptions, however, do exist. As you'll note from Illus. 30, some materials not meant for use as fencing do quite well in certain circumstances. Old wagon wheels, for example, might rot and rust because the nearly unfinished metal and the unsuitable wood are just not durable. Fortunately, such fences are entirely suitable for certain areas of the country. Arid and semiarid areas do not host high levels of either insect or fungal activity. Therefore, if constant dampness is not present to promote dry rot, almost any wood can be used as fencing material.

In areas where various kinds of rot remain a problem, use either naturally resistant wood or treat the wood to make it resistant. It is exceptionally difficult (because of chemicals' toxicity and wood's density) to make non-resistant woods durable enough to withstand over 20 years of in-ground life by treating them at home. You can, however, treat them for exposure by applying paint, preservatives, or other coatings (Illus. 56). See Table 3 for a few of the currently recommended coatings. Paints are personal choices, but any moderately good exterior house paint will do well, as will barn paint and most other exterior paints and stains (Illus. 57).

Illus. 56. ZAR clear wood preservative.

Illus. 57. Wolman wood stain and water repellent.

In-ground protection of wood in damp areas can be carried out in a number of ways, after you select the wood. Even resistant and treated varieties will benefit from proper installation methods.

Selection of materials, though, is of great importance, particularly for wood fences and can make the difference between having an attractive fence for only five years or for over three decades. Pressure-treated or naturally resistant woods will resist indefinitely decay produced by insects, fungi, or mites. Mechanical damage, then, remains the only problem, and that is dealt with by building the proper fence for the job.

Redwood is, I think, the optimum wood for fences, but in the Eastern United States it demands a high price because of current transportation costs and the dealers' preference for stocking only premium grades, such as Clear All Heart, instead of the less expensive Garden and Common grades that are just as suitable for fences. Check around for price advantages when buying redwood as a fencing material. While the finer grades may seem to be priced as high as furniture-grade walnut, the other varieties are not. In the end, too, the coloring is similar if the wood is not treated or painted. It turns a silver grey and remains that color for decades.

Cedars vary widely and are often available as small trees (Illus. 59), not much larger than bushes. The tree trunk—unsplit and untreated—makes an ideal fence post, while larger cedar trees can be easily split for use as rails. Of course cedar, like redwood, is also available in boards, though not in as many grades and often not in as many areas. Both red and white cedars are

Illus. 58. By buying Garden grades of redwood you can save money on and produce an airy look to this vertical-board fence.

suitable for fences, either as posts or as rails. Always keep in mind that the heartwood of the naturally resistant woods is the most resistant, whereas the sapwood is often no more resistant than any other wood. The most resistant woods may be needed in some areas, but I know of other areas

Illus. 59. Small cedars, such as these in my backyard, make excellent fence material. Note the overlay board on the white pasture fence near the cedars. This overlay is used to help secure board fence when the board must be placed on the side opposite the area holding the stock (a method that should never be used unless both fields are full of animals).

where cedar, used to build cabins in the 1890s in the northern United States and Europe (not the truly far northern regions, though), is still solid, looks good, and seems likely to serve for decades more even after ninety years. **Pressure-treated woods** are a good choice when constructing fences today for a very simple reason. Local species are used and are processed locally. (Various companies such as Koppers, which advertises the Wolmanizing process of pressure treating, do *not* sell wood; they are chemical companies that sell chemicals and processes, and they also advise for local distributors.) Treating local wood and selling it within the same area greatly reduces transportation costs, thus lowering the price of materials for consumers. It is much more economical to pressure-treat southern pine in Virginia than it is white pine, which is available but far less plentiful.

Pressure treating is a not-so-simple process that drives the chemical deep into the pores of the wood, where they penetrate and react with the fibres to provide superb protection. The resulting wood weathers to a silver grey similar to that of redwood and cedar.

Stakes treated as long ago as 1935 have shown no deterioration. Pressure-treated lumber retains the same basic character as the original wood but you must take a few precautions when cutting, sanding, and disposing of the waste ends. Be sure to wear a dust mask when cutting and particularly when sanding any pressure-treated material. (It's a good idea, in fact, to wear such a mask when working with any kind of wood.) Dispose of wastes in a proper manner: use a regular landfill or a trash container.

Do not burn treated-wood wastes. Almost all solutions for pressure treating woods contain one or more strong poisons, such as arsenic, while others contain substances, such as zinc, that become toxic when hot. Today, few companies still sell arsenicals, creosotes, and pentachlorphenols for treating wood at home. The chemicals cause mutations and cancer, and they must be applied with such care that home treatment is usually not practical. Limit home treatment to newer materials and processes, which require substances believed safer than the older ones.

Plain woods, such as the various pines, white and live oak, and so on, are often used in fences that will be painted or otherwise coated. They cannot, however, be used in ground contact, which requires that wood be either treated or naturally durable. There are a few characteristics to keep in mind about woods. White pine, in both treated and untreated versions, is the easiest of all to work. Southern pine is next. After that comes locust, followed by white and live oak, both of which are quite hard to work, and like locust, require pilot holes even for nailing. For greatest strength, the oaks are the obvious choice, but not always the recommended one. If the fence is to contain animals or any fast-moving objects that might strike with great speed and force from time to time, you should choose some other wood. Fencing for horses who might occasionally run into a board fence is a good example. If the impact is strong enough, the boards may break. Oak often breaks in long, spearlike slivers that could snap in such a way that it pierces the animal.

In general, you can bet on finding some form of suitable wood. It may be one of those considered here, or another type that has been treated in a manner specific to your locale, or even an untreated wood for dry areas. You may buy from a lumberyard or from a mill. Or you may locate a particular material on a one-time basis, something like railroad ties, wagon wheels, mesquite posts, or any of hundreds of other materials not generally available. Use some imagination in finding your fencing material and the results are always bound to be satisfactory (Illus. 60).

When wood fencing doesn't provide the selection needed, you must move on to other materials, such as chain-link metal fencing.

Illus. 60. Aluminum wire holds double posts firmly, forcing the rails to stay in place. Use a figure 8 loop, as shown, for best security. It is not really necessary to use such a loop at every row of rails, as is done here.

Illus. 61. Lag-screwed 2-inch-thick material attached to a very heavy post.

METAL FENCING

Chain Link is only one type of metal fencing, but it is one of the most efficient and durable types available for security and containment purposes

(Illus. 62). Although its industrial look may be unattractive, chain-link fences are popular for keeping children in yards, pets in runs, and for providing security around homes, pools, and other areas. It is relatively easy to install, since shops that sell the equipment also loan installation kits. It comes in a variety of prices, depending on strength and height.

Illus. 62. Chain-link fence.

When planning the installation of a chain-link fence, first figure the height you need. A 4-foot-high fence will contain small children and provide some security; 6 feet high is better for moderate security; 8 feet high is best for surrounding a swimming pool and for greater security. When selecting wire thickness, remember that the smaller the gauge number the thicker (and more expensive) the wire. The larger the mesh opening is in the chain link, the cheaper the fence will be. Tight security requires a mesh as small as 1¾ inches. Line posts for residential use are smaller than termination posts, usually measuring about 1⅝ inches on the outside diameter. Corner or termination posts are about ¼ inch larger. The top rail measurement varies with the manufacturer but is usually at least 1¼ inches in diameter.

Choose the frame for a chain-link gate according to the width the gate must span. Frame sizes may vary from your basic fence size. For a gate on a wide (over 10 feet particularly) drive you will probably have to erect a double-door gate. Gates for people usually match standard sizes with no problem.

Other types of metal fencing, including metal combined with wood fencing, abound. Of course, *chicken mesh* that measures 4 feet high is often used to surround gardens. Like all metal that is not vinyl coated or enamelled, it must be well galvanized to withstand the weather. Various kinds of *diamond-mesh* fences are available and are often combined with board fencing, especially with a board top rail, for horse fencing. *Barbed wire* comes in many styles and weights for stock fencing and is suitable usually for all but horse fencing. (Check with your local authorities, though, before completing plans for any stock fencing, including horse fencing; they will have the latest information on methods and uses of materials.) *Straight-wire* fences that are erected between steel or wooden fence posts are not often used these days because they have to be awfully heavy to stop any animal or to provide security. Usually, wire used in such a manner requires a mesh, or weave, of some sort. Many kinds are available. Straight-wire fencing is most appropriate for electric fencing, which is probably the cheapest method of holding stock within a large area.

The transformers used to electrify the wire are rated according to the number of miles (10 to 15 miles usually) of fencing that can be charged with one transformer. Cost of the transformer is relatively low, as is the cost of the simple wire. Active animals might need a double strand, while less active animals need only a single strand. Place the strands low enough to keep the animals from crawling underneath and high enough to keep them from stepping over. Hanging a rag or an aluminum pie plate every 10 to 15 feet from the wire enables you to see the wire before you bump into it with bare flesh or wet clothing.

Posts for an electric fence may be made of fibreglass, metal, or wood. Those of fibreglass need no insulators and can simply be driven into the ground with a heavy hammer; those of metal need insulators, but can also be driven into the ground with a heavy hammer; and those of wood may or may not require insulators and can be installed by driving or setting the post into postholes. An electric fence also makes an inexpensive and effective temporary stock fence when erected with fibreglass posts.

You may wish to try some locally available materials that become abundant for one reason or another. If a builder, for example, buys too much PVC (polyvinylchloride) pipe in a size you need as well as a lot of T fittings, you might be able to purchase them at far below their normal price. If your locale abounds in cedar trees that are larger than the post size, you might wish to fell several and split them yourself to use as rails in a zigzag fence, or post and rails in a post-and-rail fence. Cedar and most pines are not difficult to split. Simply swing the splitting maul at the butt of the felled log to create a crack. Slip in one 5-pound wedge and hammer it into the butt. Move a few feet down the crack formed in the side of the log and hammer in another 5-pound wedge. When that one goes down far enough, the first will be free. Just keep step-wedging down the log until it pops open.

HARDWARE

Fence hardware these days could occupy almost an entire book of its own. I'll not make any attempt to cover it completely but will describe generally what you will, or may, need to erect a fence with durable gates that open and close correctly.

First, of course, comes the old carpentry standby, nails. Without them, nothing much would get built these days, and fences are no exception. To prevent corrosion in wood fences, use either nails made of aluminum or those that have been galvanized, preferably through the hot-dip method, which produces a heavier, less porous coating. Mild steel nails are fine. Offhand, I can't think of a single fencing job that needs a hardened nail.

Nails used to attach boards to posts should be three times longer than the width of the board being attached, so that a nominal 1-inch board, which is actually ¾ inch thick, would require a nail 2¼ inches long. Since 7d nails are hard to find, use an 8d nail. A full-size 1-inch-thick board would require a 10d nail, which is 3 inches long.

Aluminum nails may seem more expensive than hot-dipped galvanized nails, but it's an illusion. First, there are three times as many aluminum nails of a particular size in a pound than there are steel ones. Second, galvanized nails cost considerably more than plain-finished nails. My only objection to aluminum nails is that certain sizes are difficult to find and they bend more easily than do steel nails. Oddly enough, the fact that aluminum nails bend more easily than steel is in their favor in hardwood fencing. Because you have to drill a pilot hole for *any* nail in most hardwoods, inserting aluminum nails into the drilled hole is easy, and prevents them from bending so easily.

Lag screws, carriage bolts, washers, and other fasteners must also be coated in order to prevent rust (Illus. 63–66). They're probably available in aluminum, but I haven't been able to find any locally.

Illus. 63. Nickel-plated gate latch is heavy, serviceable.

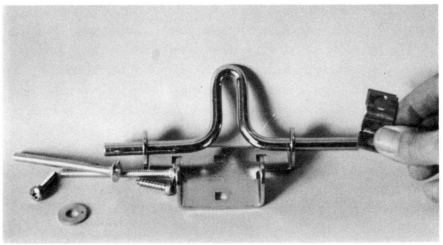

Illus. 64. This simple gate pull works well with a friction fit and with gates using other forms of latches.

Illus. 65. Stanley's more complex thumb-latch gate pull requires no additional parts.

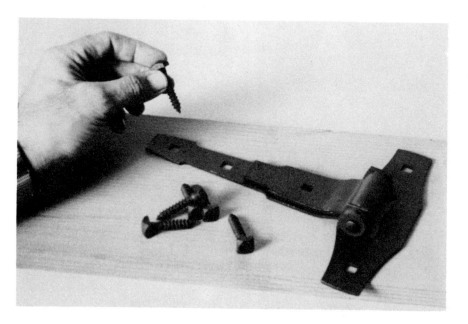

Illus. 66. Note the unusual lag screws that were made for this very heavy-duty spring-loaded gate hinge.

Several companies, like TECO, make anchors that are galvanized enough for use outdoors even though their primary use is indoors. I've used them in decks, fences, and roofs. They cost somewhat more than standard fasteners, but because the better brands come with their own special nails, the added cost is not very high, and the labor saved can be great. They also significantly increase the strength in some constructions.

Gate hardware comes in a multitude of forms, and you will find detailed information in Chapter 11, page 111.

8 · Tools

No matter what kind of fence you construct, proper tools of good quality will make the job much easier. If the tools seem too expensive to buy for a one-time use, then rent them. A great many companies will loan certain fence-installation tools—wire stretchers, for instance—when you buy the major portion of materials from them.

Because most fences are made of wood or a combination of wood and other materials, the primary tools for fence erection are the same as for any other form of carpentry: saws, drills, drill bits, hammers. Specialized tools such as posthole diggers are essential for a neat and strong installation, and the manual digger is relatively inexpensive (Illus. 67). Power posthole augers

Illus. 67. This Jackson contractor's wheelbarrow holds about 5 cubic feet of gravel, cement, or other loose material and is very handy. The True Temper posthole digger is the heavy-duty model, designed for digging in heavy red clay. If you install much fencing material or do other outdoor work, be sure to buy tools that will last long enough to justify your purchase.

save time and energy when erecting a large installation in hard soil. But since they are readily available for rent, buying one isn't necessary.

SAWS

Handsaws for cutting fencing material include the panel, or standard, handsaw, and the best buy probably is one with 8 or 10 teeth per inch (Illus. 68). Finer toothed saws are available, but the 8 or 10 teeth-per-inch saws give a fairly fine cut and make the work go faster. Look for a handsaw with a handle that fits your hand well and for a blade that feels well balanced.

Illus. 68. A 10-point (teeth-per-inch) crosscut saw.

The blade should be taper ground and should fall in at least the middle range of quality in any manufacturer's line. There is almost certainly no need to buy a hand ripsaw, so the crosscut model will do fine. If you need to ripsaw some fence stock, use a circular saw, at least, and preferably a table saw, because you will get too tired operating the handsaw.

Keyhole and compass saws (Illus. 69) are good for making small-curves and larger cutouts in fence materials. These are relatively cheap saws, often

Illus. 69. Compass and key-hole saws are handy for making noncritical curves and for correcting small mistakes.

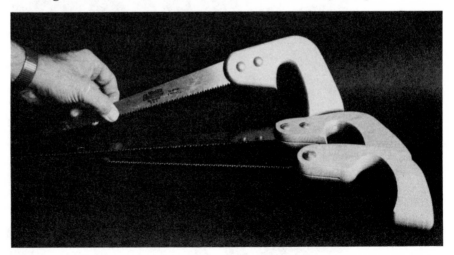

offered as part of a "nest" of saws, which contain pruning blades as well. Blades are generally replaceable but hard to find. You need them only if you want to make a number of inside cuts of modest size in the fence.

For fancy picket-fence designs, you might want to use a coping saw, though either a jigsaw or band saw would do a faster, neater job.

Hacksaws (Illus. 70) range widely in price. If your only use for such a saw is to cut a few pieces of pipe for a fence, the middle range saws are fine. If

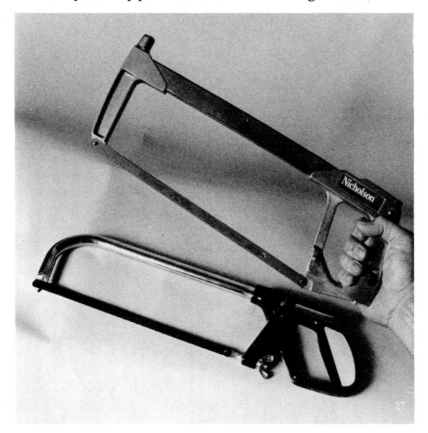

Illus. 70. The hacksaw at top is Nicholson's top of the line model, while the other is Stanley's middle of the line.

more work is to be done on metal, now or later, choose one of the best quality saws. See Illus. 71 for instructions on hand sawing.

POWER SAWS

Modern power saws can drastically reduce the amount of work required to construct a fence. I seriously doubt you'll need, or even want, to purchase a table or radial arm saw just for one fence installation, but you will certainly need a circular saw with a blade with a 7¼-inch or 6½-inch diameter (Illus. 72).

When selecting such a saw, keep in mind that the widest variety of both blade types and saws is available in the 7¼-inch size. Also consider the amount of sawing you must do for this and any future job you might tackle. If the fence to be installed is relatively small in both height and length, a

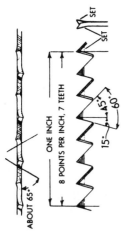

SET

SET

ONE INCH

8 POINTS PER INCH, 7 TEETH

15° 45° 60°

ABOUT 65°

CROSS CUT SAW TEETH ARE LIKE KNIFE POINTS. THEY CUT LIKE TWO ROWS OF KNIFE POINTS AND CRUMBLE OUT THE WOOD BETWEEN THE CUTS.

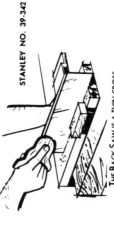

45°

45°

STANLEY NO. 39-342

ABOUT 45° IS THE CORRECT ANGLE BETWEEN THE SAW AND THE WORK FOR CROSS CUT SAWING.

THE BACK SAW IS A THIN CROSS CUT SAW WITH FINE TEETH, STIFFENED BY A THICK BACK. A POPULAR SIZE IS 12" WITH 14 PTS PER INCH. IT IS USED FOR FINE ACCURATE WORK.

EDUCATIONAL DEPARTMENT
CHART NO. 19
BY R O REGER

HANDLE

HEEL

BACK

TEETH

BLADE

TOE

STANLEY NO. 39-108

THE SIZE OF A SAW IS DETERMINED BY THE LENGTH OF THE BLADE IN INCHES. SOME POPULAR SIZES ARE 24" AND 26". THE COARSENESS OR FINENESS OF A SAW IS DETERMINED BY THE NUMBER OF POINTS PER INCH.
A COARSE SAW IS BETTER FOR FAST WORK AND FOR GREEN WOOD.
A FINE SAW IS BETTER FOR SMOOTH ACCURATE CUTTING AND FOR DRY SEASONED WOOD.
5-1/2 AND 6 POINTS ARE IN COMMON USE FOR RIP SAWS.
7 AND 8 POINTS ARE IN COMMON USE FOR CROSS CUT SAWS.
SAW TEETH ARE SET, EVERY OTHER TOOTH IS BENT TO THE RIGHT AND THOSE BETWEEN TO THE LEFT, TO MAKE THE KERF WIDER THAN THE SAW.
THIS PREVENTS THE SAW FROM BINDING IN THE KERF OR SAW CUT.
QUALITY SAWS IN ADDITION ARE TAPER GROUND, BEING THINNER AT THE BACK THAN AT THE TOOTHED EDGE.
KEEP SAW TEETH SHARP AND PROPERLY SET.

KERF

CORRECT LENGTH

MEASUREMENT

WASTE | A | WASTE

CORRECT

MEASUREMENT

WASTE | B | WASTE

MEASUREMENT

WASTE | C | WASTE

PIECE TOO SHORT

WASTE | D | WASTE

SPACE TOO LARGE

BE SURE TO SAW CAREFULLY ON THE WASTE SIDE OF THE LINE AS AT A AND B. SAWING ON THE LINE OR ON THE WRONG SIDE OF THE LINE MAKES THE STOCK TOO SHORT AS AT C OR THE OPENING TOO LARGE AS SHOWN AT D.

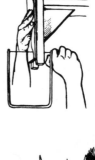

THE COPING SAW IS USED TO CUT IRREGULAR SHAPES AND INTRICATELY CURVED PATTERNS IN THIN WOOD.
STANLEY NO. 39-106

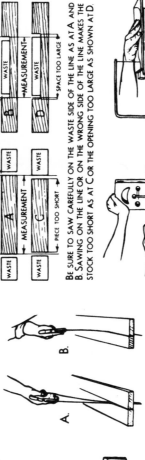

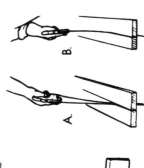

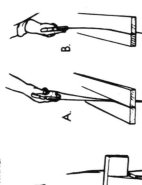

COMPASS OR KEYHOLE SAWS ARE USED TO CUT CURVED OR STRAIGHT SIDED HOLES.
STANLEY NO. 175C

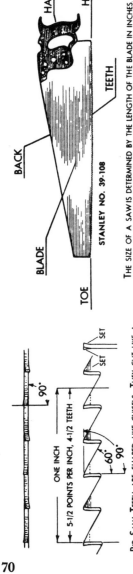

90°

ONE INCH

5-1/2 POINTS PER INCH, 4-1/2 TEETH

SET

SET

60° 90°

RIP SAW TEETH ARE SHAPED LIKE CHISELS. THEY CUT LIKE A GANG OF CHISELS IN A ROW.

60°

ABOUT 60° IS THE CORRECT ANGLE BETWEEN THE SAW AND THE WORK FOR RIP SAWING.

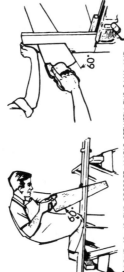

B.

A.

A. IF THE SAW LEAVES THE LINE TWIST THE HANDLE SLIGHTLY AND DRAW IT BACK TO THE LINE.
B. IF THE SAW IS NOT SQUARE TO THE STOCK, BEND IT A LITTLE AND GRADUALLY STRAIGHTEN IT. BE CAREFUL NOT TO PERMANENTLY BEND OR KINK THE BLADE.

90°

START THE SAW CUT BY DRAWING THE SAW BACKWARD. HOLD THE BLADE SQUARE TO THE STOCK. STEADY IT AT THE LINE WITH THE THUMB

STANLEY TOOLS
NEW BRITAIN, CONN., U.S.A.
COPYRIGHT 1968

Illus. 71. How to use handsaws.

middle-range consumer-model saw should serve you well, but if the work load is heavy, you'll want to at least investigate the professional-model saws (Illus. 73).

There are major differences, other than price, between professional and consumer circular saws. In fact, the price for the professional model without

Illus. 72. Larger, stationary tools such as this Shopsmith Mark V can often speed pre-erection work a great deal, but are not truly essential for fence building. Cutting picket tops on my Shopsmith Mark V.

Illus. 73. Note the large control knobs on this Black & Decker professional-model 7¼-inch circular saw.

fancy features may well begin where the consumer models with fancy (and often not very useful) features end. The professional saw has a longer cord to facilitate cutting 8-foot panels of plywood, and it is made as a two-piece set for ease of replacement. It is also much heavier and manufactured with better materials.

In addition, the professional saw is more accurately machined than the consumer model, and the bearings are of a better type and quality, all of which enables the engine to operate at cooler temperatures. With such a cooler running machine you can get more power, and the saw will last longer. Heavier-duty switches protect better against dust, and a helpful aid, such as a drop foot, is usually available. A drop-foot saw has a base plate that drops straight down, facilitating adjustment for cut depth. The base plate is also heavier, and the control and adjustment knobs are larger (Illus. 74).

Illus. 74. This Porter Cable saw uses computer chips to regulate blade speed and has the heaviest-duty motor I've ever seen in a nongear-driven saw—14.5 amperes. It is a pro model, and the cost reflects the features, but the saw is well worth the money. Note how the large knobs and top handle provide ease of control on this Porter Cable saw during a long cut.

If you plan to make a top picket design using anything other than mitre cuts, then consider a jig saw (Illus. 75). If you plan a large fence, then choose

Illus. 75. This Craftsman jigsaw, from Sears, Roebuck, offers computer-chip speed control which produces smoother cuts.

a professional model, which will share many of the features of the professional circular saw (although not its drop-foot base plate). Such saws, with the correct blade inserted, can make all sorts of fancy and not-so-fancy cuts, as well as fairly decent straight cuts. In general, look for ease of handling and a variable-speed motor. Even professional models today come with variable speed, and some have computer chips to hold the speed at a particular level. The heavier, professional models make complex cuts easy because vibration is lower, too (Illus. 76).

There are a number of other power saws that might be helpful in working with fences, including table saws and chain saws. Neither is an

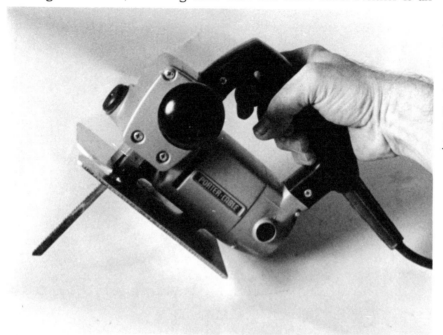

Illus. 76. You'll note, on this professional model jigsaw, the large control knob and the thick base plate. Control with the variable-speed trigger is superb, and vibration is very low compared to other jigsaws.

item you should consider purchasing if you plan to build only one fence, unless the fence is exceptionally large. Both saws are readily available for rent, though. A reciprocating saw might be handy in replacing and repair-

Illus. 77. This Black & Decker compound mitre saw performs almost as well as a radial saw and costs far less. It's easy to set up and has a unique blade guard that is truly excellent. For cutting anything from picture frames to house mouldings, this is the saw to get.

ing a fence, but in fence building it is somewhat less suitable than the circular saw, except for trimming posts or rails that measure more than 2½ inches thick.

DRILLS

Some styles of board fences require no hardware at all, so you don't need a drill. But to install gate hardware, antisag hardware, or any other fixtures, you will probably need a drill.

One of the great improvements in tools today is the cordless drill (Illus. 78). Some years ago I paid a small fortune for one of the first models. It

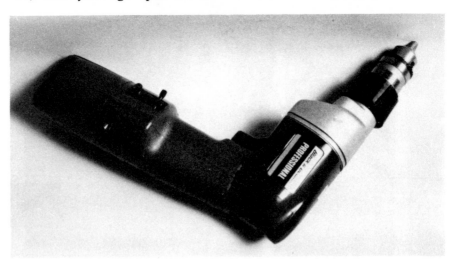

Illus. 78. This Black & Decker cordless drill and screwdriver has a clutch, which means it can be used in almost any material.

took sixteen to twenty-four hours to charge, did not have a separate power pack, and burned out in three months. Today, all my cordless drills have separate power packs and quick battery chargers that bring the drill to full capacity in one or two hours. Several years ago, fencing part of what was to be a polo training field, I used my old cordless drill to make ⅛-inch pilot holes in white oak boards. After eighty-five or ninety holes, the drill was dead. Today, I could take my new drill and three charged packs out there and put in nearly 1,000 pilot holes before it would need a recharge, though, of course, one pack could be kept on charge when it went dead.

As with saws, look for a drill that fits your hand well and that feels well balanced (Illus. 79). If possible, choose a professional model, and I recommend getting a clutched model and a straight drive model. If you must choose between the two make your main drill a clutched model. Drills made with clutches can accommodate screwdrivers as well (Illus. 80). Of course, choosing one with variable speed is sensible, too, for it prevents the bits from "walking" when you start drilling holes. A walking drill bit is one that wanders away from the spot where it is supposed to start the hole when the drill is turned on; center punching the mark is the standard way of

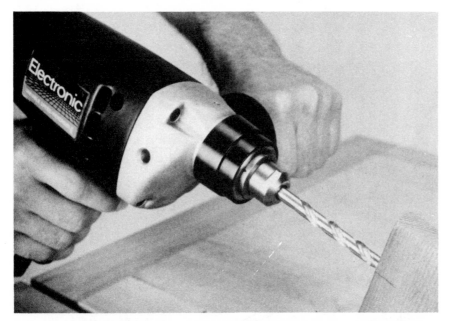

Illus. 79. Again, computer chips help maintain a steady drilling speed for a particular material, so there is less strain on the drill itself and on the drill bit.

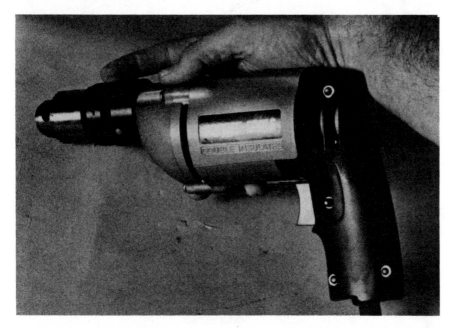

Illus. 80. This professional-model Porter Cable drill has a clutch and a ³⁄₈-inch chuck that works beautifully as a screwdriver as well. It is not cordless, so you will need a long extension cord when working on an outside fence.

preventing such walking, but a slow, steady start with a variable-speed drill will also work. A ³⁄₈-inch-capacity drill chuck is better because it can use a wider variety of accessories than the ¼-inch.

For heavier work, or for work closer to electrical outlets, choose a good ½-inch drill. Here, a consumer model should suffice for most people. Select one with a *D* handle to facilitate exertion of a lot of pressure on the bit. Pistol-handled drills are for lighter work. For extremely heavy work—as in drilling holes for lead anchors in a masonry wall so that you can attach a fence to it—you will probably want to rent a heavy-duty ½-inch or larger drill. (See also Illus. 81 for instructions on operating a hand drill.)

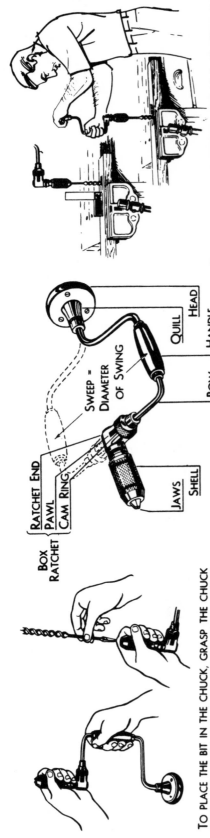

TO BORE A VERTICAL HOLE, HOLD THE BRACE AND BIT PERPENDICULAR TO THE SURFACE OF THE WORK. TEST BY SIGHT. COMPARE THE DIRECTION OF THE BIT TO THE NEAREST STRAIGHT EDGE OR TO SIDES OF THE VISE. A TRY SQUARE MAY BE HELD NEAR THE BIT.

TO BORE A HORIZONTAL HOLE, HOLD THE HEAD OF THE BRACE CUPPED IN THE LEFT HAND AGAINST THE STOMACH AND WITH THE THUMB AND FOREFINGER AROUND THE QUILL TO BORE THRU WITHOUT SPLINTERING THE SECOND FACE, STOP WHEN THE SCREW POINT IS THRU AND FINISH FROM THE SECOND FACE. WHEN BORING THRU WITH AN EXPANSIVE BIT IT IS BEST TO CLAMP A PIECE OF WOOD TO THE SECOND FACE AND BORE STRAIGHT THRU.

EDUCATIONAL DEPARTMENT
CHART NO. 26
BY R O REGER

BOX RATCHET
RATCHET END
PAWL
CAM RING

SWEEP = DIAMETER OF SWING

HEAD
QUILL
HANDLE
BOW
SHELL
JAWS

STANLEY RATCHET BIT BRACE No 923-10 IN SWEEP

TO OPERATE THE RATCHET TURN THE CAM RING. TURNING THE CAM RING TO THE RIGHT WILL ALLOW THE BIT TO TURN RIGHT AND GIVE RATCHET ACTION WHEN THE HANDLE IS TURNED LEFT. TURN THE CAM RING LEFT TO REVERSE THE ACTION. THE RATCHET BRACE IS INDISPENSABLE WHEN BORING A HOLE IN A CORNER OR WHERE SOME OBJECT PREVENTS MAKING A FULL TURN WITH THE HANDLE.

TO PLACE THE BIT IN THE CHUCK, GRASP THE CHUCK SHELL AND TURN THE HANDLE TO THE LEFT UNTIL THE JAWS ARE WIDE OPEN. INSERT THE BIT SHANK IN THE SQUARE SOCKET AT THE BOTTOM OF THE CHUCK AND TURN THE HANDLE TO THE RIGHT UNTIL THE BIT IS HELD FIRMLY IN THE JAWS.

BIT BRACE CHUCKS OF THE ABOVE DESIGN, WITHOUT A SQUARE SOCKET ARE OPERATED IN LIKE MANNER. THE CORNERS OF THE TAPER SHANK OF THE BIT SHOULD BE CAREFULLY SEATED AND CENTERED IN THE V GROOVES OF THE JAWS.

STANLEY TOOLS
NEW BRITAIN, CONN. U.S.A.
COPYRIGHT 1966

Illus. 81. Using a bit brace.

DRILL BITS AND ACCESSORIES

The list of accessories for the common electric drill has become so long that it could almost constitute a catalog itself. From paint mixers to nail spinners (to drive brads or other small nails without splitting wood), the attachments are so varied it sometimes seems that just because most home-owners have an electric drill, someone thought he had to devise a new use for the thing every week.

Drill bits are the most common accessory and come in a variety of styles to suit different materials and uses. Hammer drills and masonry drills require carbide-tipped bits. In addition, the bits themselves are shaped differently. Spade bits, designed entirely for boring wood for rough work, are just flat pieces of steel, spread to size and are usually made with a biting spur in the middle. Twist bits are made for drilling into wood or metal and are named after the winding indentation that wraps around the bit. They have a moderately blunt point, drill a cleaner hole than spade bits, and have a greater tendency to "walk" during their initial entrance into a material. Usually, twist drill bits are available in ¾-inch or smaller sizes, while spade bits can be as large as 1½-inches. Twist drill bits over ¼ inch in diameter often have reduced shanks to fit small drill chucks (Illus. 82).

Brad-point drill bits are more precise than the twist bits and are far more costly than either spade or twist drill bits, but they look like the twist drill bit more than anything else. They are available in sizes up to about 1 inch. They're seldom needed for the relatively rough carpentry of fence building. You will probably not need a bit any more precise than the brad-point drill bit for any of the work covered in this book (Illus. 82).

Screwdriver tips are probably the next most common accessory for electric drills. Again, the variety is great and the quality range is fairly wide. Tips are now available to fit slotted, Phillips head, and several newer, high-contact screw-head styles. Length of the tips varies, and I find that the longer the tip, the better its quality. A tip short enough to disappear inside a drill chuck is almost sure to be difficult to adjust. If you are doing extensive work that requires screws, you'll find that today's brass screws with Phillips heads (or other high-torque head designs) are readily available in thread styles that drive easily under power. These are similar to the familiar dark-coated wallboard screws but are not prone to rust damage (Illus. 83).

Other accessories include countersinks and counterbores. Usually, it's far faster to use something, such as a ScrewMate, that simultaneously provides the countersink, counterbore, and a pilot hole for a specified screw size than to do the job in three stages with three different tools.

Here is a tip for drilling pilot holes and then power driving screws into those holes. The work goes much faster if, after drilling the pilot holes with a single-speed drill, you use a clutched drill with screwdriver tip to insert

TWIST BITS, 32NDS OF AN INCH

$\frac{8}{32}$ $\frac{6}{32}$

FORSTNER BITS 16THS

$\frac{12}{16}$

AUGER BITS 16THS OF AN INCH

$\frac{12}{16}$ $\frac{8}{16}$ $\frac{6}{16}$

$\frac{3}{8}''$ $\frac{1}{2}''$ $\frac{3}{4}''$ $\frac{3}{16}''$ $\frac{1}{4}''$

BITS ARE MARKED FOR SIZE BY A SINGLE NUMBER THE NUMERATOR OF THE FRACTION STANDS FOR THE DIAMETER OF THE BIT AUGER AND FORSTNER BITS ARE MARKED BY 16THS OF AN INCH NO 8 STANDS FOR 8/16' OR 1/2' TWIST BITS FOR WOOD ARE USUALLY MARKED IN THE SAME WAY, BY 32NDS OF AN INCH NO 8 STANDS FOR 8/32' OR 1/4'

STANLEY BIT GAUGE NO 47

AN ADJUSTABLE BIT GAUGE MAY BE USED TO REGULATE THE DEPTH OF HOLES

EXPANSIVE BIT NO 71 A

THE EXPANSIVE BIT TAKES THE PLACE OF MANY LARGE BITS THE CUTTER MAY BE ADJUSTED FOR VARIOUS SIZED HOLES MOVING THE CUTTER ADJUSTING SCREW ONE COMPLETE TURN ENLARGES OR REDUCES THE HOLE 1/8' ONE HALF TURN 1/16' TEST THE SIZE ON A PIECE OF WASTE WOOD FOR BORING THROUGH, CLAMP A PIECE OF WASTE WOOD ON THE BACK OF THE WORK TO PREVENT SPLITTING

EDUCATIONAL DEPARTMENT CHART NO. 23
BY R O REGER

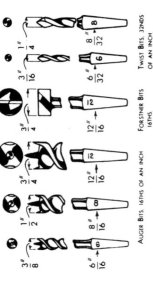

TANG

SHANK

TWIST

SPUR

SPUR

CUTTING EDGE

FEED SCREW

CUTTING EDGE

AUGER BIT NO 100RJ

AUGER BITS ARE SIZED BY 16THS OF AN INCH, MEASURING THE DIAMETER BITS VARY IN LENGTH FROM 7' TO 10' DOWEL BITS ARE SHORT AUGER BITS ABOUT 5' LONG

THE DIAMOND POINT IS USED FOR MACHINE BORING WITH POWER FEED

THE SINGLE THREAD FEED SCREW IS BEST FOR FAST CUTTING IN GREEN OR GUMMY WOOD

THE STANDARD DOUBLE THREAD FEED SCREW IS BEST FOR GENERAL WORK WITH SEASONED WOOD IT IS PREFERRED FOR CABINET AND PATTERN MAKING

SHARPEN THE CUTTING EDGES ON THE TOP TO MAINTAIN THE CLEARANCE ON THE UNDER SIDE THE CUTTING EDGES MUST BE KEPT EVEN

SHARPEN AUGER BITS WITH A BIT FILE FOR A KEEN EDGE, ALSO WHET FOR A SLIPSTONE SHARPEN THE SPURS ON THE INSIDE TO PRESERVE THE DIAMETER

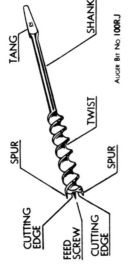

BRAD AWLS ARE USED TO MAKE HOLES FOR SMALL SCREWS AND NAILS. TO AVOID SPLITTING THE WOOD, START THE AWL WITH ITS EDGE ACROSS THE GRAIN, TURNING IT BACK AND FORTH SLIGHTLY AS YOU PRESS DOWN DO NOT LET THE EDGE COME PARALLEL WITH THE GRAIN

TWIST BITS FOR WOOD ARE USED TO MAKE HOLES FOR SCREWS, NAILS OR BOLTS. THEY ARE SIZED BY 32NDS OF AN INCH AND RANGE FROM NO 2-1/16' AND LARGER

BIT STOCK DRILLS ARE DESIGNED AND TEMPERED TO MAKE HOLES IN METAL, BUT MAY ALSO BE USED IN WOOD, ESPECIALLY IN REPAIR WORK WHERE CONTACT WITH NAILS OR METAL IS POSSIBLE THEY ARE SIZED BY 32NDS OF AN INCH AND RANGE FROM NO 2 = 1/16' AND LARGER

STANLEY COUNTERSINK NO 139 FOR BIT BRACES

STANLEY COUNTERSINK NO 137 FOR HAND DRILLS

COUNTERSINK BITS ARE USED TO WIDEN SCREW HOLES SO THAT THE HEADS OF FLAT-HEAD SCREWS MAY BE FLUSH, OR SLIGHTLY BELOW, THE SURFACE OF THE WORK

FORSTNER BITS ARE USED TO BORE HOLES PARTWAY THROUGH WHERE THE AUGER BIT SCREW OR SPUR WOULD GO THROUGH THE WORK, ALSO ON END GRAIN, THIN WOOD, OR NEAR AN END WHERE AN AUGER BIT WOULD SPLIT THE WORK TO CENTER OR START A FORSTNER BIT, SCRIBE A CIRCLE THE SIZE OF THE HOLE WITH DIVIDERS AND PRESS THE RIM OF THE FORSTNER BIT INTO IT FORSTNER BITS ARE SIZED BY 16THS OF AN INCH FROM NO 4-1/4' AND LARGER

STANLEY TOOLS
NEW BRITAIN, CONN., U.S.A.
COPYRIGHT 1964

Illus. 82. Using drill bits.

the screws. Using the clutched and straight-drive drills enables you to work continuously without having to change bits every few minutes.

Other drill accessories may become helpful as you move along, but simply concentrating on these two types of drills will save you a great deal of trouble over time. Use carbide-tipped bits for masonry and rough work, and regular steel bits for other work. Be sure to look for high-quality tools any time you go to buy such items.

HAMMERS

Carpenter's hammers are available in a number of handle materials and head weights (Illus. 84). This is one tool on which it does not pay to even think of economizing, for the difference between the worst and the best hammer on the market is nominal. But the difference in the way they perform is great.

Handle materials include wood, fibreglass, and steel. Steel handles may be solid or hollow, and I think the hollow one performs somewhat more easily. A neoprene shock pad will fit your hand snugly, as it will on any fibreglass handle you select. Fibreglass handles are my favorite, since they seem to be nearly as strong as steel and as shock-absorbent as wood. Wood is the oldest handle material, of course, and is sometimes sneered at today, which is slightly silly. It makes a fine handle if, like any other material, it is properly formed and installed. Wood-handled hammers tend to cost a bit less for equivalent head quality than do those of steel and fibreglass, but the difference is negligible.

Illus. 84. Fibreglass-handled carpenter's hammer. Use the proper grip on your claw hammer. It's not a baseball bat so choking up won't improve your aim.

I suggest you find some way to try all three types of handles when selecting your own hammer. Also consider the head weight, which may range from about 13 ounces to 32 ounces. The first is too light for fence work, and the latter is too heavy for most people for standard work. It's meant for rough framing, as are the 22-ounce, 24-ounce, and 28-ounce hammers. For most fence building and home projects, you'll almost certainly want a 16- or 20-ounce head with a standard-length handle. For heavier fencing work, you may prefer the 20- or even 22-ounce head with a 15-inch handle. When choosing a hammer, consider the fact that most people prefer a 16-ounce head no matter how strong they are. A few use 20 ounces, as I do, but as elbow joints age, sometimes it is easier to use the lighter weight one. (A heavier hammer, however, when handled properly can drive nails with more ease than a lighter one can.)

Fine finish, carefully cut claws, and a solidly installed handle are signs of quality. The shape of the claws may be straight (rip) or curved (most common). Some people claim the curved-claw hammer balances better. It seems to me to make no difference at all as long as the hammer is well made and balanced.

Of course, claw hammers aren't the only style available or necessary for erecting fences. For very heavy spiking or securing tight-fitting (rough only) joints you might prefer an engineer's hammer. Use a sledgehammer or an engineer's hammer to drive in stakes and posts. For tight-fitting wood joints where marring the surface might be a problem, consider the Stanley Tool Company's extensive line of CompoCast hammers. These are made of a dense, strong plastic, with shot-loaded heads that deaden the blows as they land, helping to prevent hammer bounce.

SCREWDRIVERS

Another nearly essential tool is the screwdriver, which most people have around the house in several forms. Tip styles are less important than the way the handle fits in your hand, the way the tip fits into the screw, and quality of finish. The tip style of the screwdriver, obviously, must match the head style of the screws you use. (Try to employ no more than two—it saves confusion.) And to prevent the tip from constantly slipping out of the screwhead because of poor fit, be sure to match the head size. Remember, even Phillips screws come in several sizes (No. 0, 1, 2, etc.), though some of the newer high-torque versions don't (Illus. 85).

To increase speed without using a power screwdriver, use the Yankee ratcheting model, which is a proven tool and comes in several tip styles and

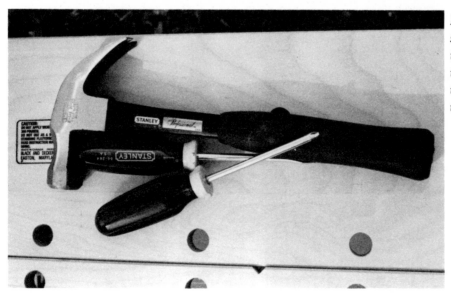

Illus. 85. The Phillips and slotted screwdrivers here have the wedge-shaped handles that have become popular in the past decade. They do fit the hand well.

SELECT A SCREW DRIVER OF LENGTH AND TIP FITTED TO THE WORK.
SCREW DRIVERS ARE SPECIFIED BY THE LENGTH OF THE BLADE.
THE TIP SHOULD BE STRAIGHT AND NEARLY PARALLEL SIDED. IT SHOULD ALSO FIT THE SCREW SLOT AND BE NOT WIDER THAN THE SCREW HEAD.

IF THE TIP IS TOO WIDE IT WILL SCAR THE WOOD AROUND THE SCREW HEAD
IF THE SCREW DRIVER IS NOT HELD IN LINE WITH THE SCREW IT WILL SLIP OUT OF THE SLOT AND MAR BOTH THE SCREW AND THE WORK.

IF THE TIP IS ROUNDED OR BEVELED IT WILL RAISE OUT OF THE SLOT SPOILING THE SCREW HEAD. REGRIND OR FILE THE TIP TO MAKE IT AS SHOWN ABOVE

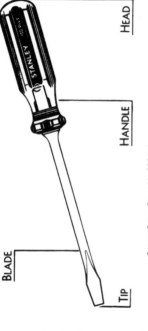

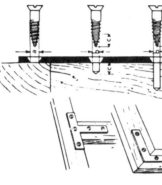

USE THE LONGEST SCREW DRIVER CONVENIENT FOR THE WORK. MORE POWER CAN BE APPLIED TO A LONG SCREW DRIVER THAN A SHORT ONE, WITH LESS DANGER OF ITS SLIPPING OUT OF THE SLOT
HOLD THE HANDLE FIRMLY IN THE PALM OF THE RIGHT HAND WITH THE THUMB AND FOREFINGER GRASPING THE HANDLE NEAR THE FERRULE. WITH THE LEFT HAND STEADY THE TIP AND KEEP IT PRESSED INTO THE SLOT WHILE RENEWING THE GRIP ON THE HANDLE FOR A NEW TURN

IF NO HOLE IS BORED FOR THE THREADED PART OF THE SCREW THE WOOD IS OFTEN SPLIT OR THE SCREW IS TWISTED OFF
IF A SCREW TURNS TOO HARD, BACK IT OUT AND ENLARGE THE HOLE
A LITTLE SOAP ON THE THREADS OF THE SCREW MAKES IT EASIER TO DRIVE

TO FASTEN HINGES OR OTHER HARDWARE IN PLACE WITH SCREWS:
1. LOCATE THE POSITION OF THE PIECE OF HARDWARE ON THE WORK.
2. RECESS THE WORK TO RECEIVE THE HARDWARE, IF IT IS NECESSARY
3. LOCATE THE POSITIONS OF THE SCREWS
4. SELECT SCREWS THAT WILL EASILY PASS THRU THE HOLES IN THE HARDWARE, AS AT a
5. BORE THE PILOT HOLES (SECOND HOLE) SLIGHTLY SMALLER THAN THE DIAMETER OF THE THREADED PART OF THE SCREWS, AS AT b
6. DRIVE THE SCREWS TIGHTLY IN PLACE
IF THE WOOD IS SOFT, BORE AS DEEP AS HALF THE LENGTH OF THE THREADED PART OF THE SCREW, AS AT c. IF THE WOOD IS HARD, (OAK), THE SCREW SOFT (BRASS), OR IF THE SCREW IS LARGE, THE HOLE MUST BE NEARLY AS DEEP AS THE SCREW, AS AT d. HOLES FOR SMALL SCREWS ARE USUALLY MADE WITH BRAD AWLS

EDUCATIONAL DEPARTMENT
CHART NO. 21
BY R O REGER

DETERMINE SCREW SHANK SIZES BY COMPARISON BELOW

No. 1 2 3 4 5 6 7 8
9 10 12 14 16 18

HANDLE   BLADE   TIP   HEAD

STANLEY SCREW DRIVER NO. 1006-6 IN. BLADE

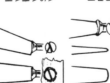

TO FASTEN TWO PIECES OF WOOD TOGETHER WITH SCREWS:
1. LOCATE THE POSITIONS OF THE SCREW HOLES.
2. BORE THE FIRST HOLE SLIGHTLY SMALLER THAN THE THREADED PART OF THE SCREW THROUGH BOTH PIECES OF WOOD AS AT b. BORE ONLY AS DEEP AS THREE QUARTERS THE LENGTH OF THE SCREW.
3. BORE THE SECOND HOLE IN THE FIRST PIECE OF WOOD SLIGHTLY LARGER THAN THE DIAMETER OF THE SCREW SHANK, AS AT a.
4. COUNTERSINK THE FIRST HOLES TO MATCH THE DIAMETER OF THE HEADS OF THE SCREWS, AS AT c.
5. DRIVE THE SCREWS TIGHTLY IN PLACE WITH THE SCREW DRIVERS.

FLAT HEAD — LENGTH
ROUND HEAD — LENGTH
OVAL HEAD — LENGTH

STANLEY TOOLS
NEW BRITAIN, CONN. U.S.A.
COPYRIGHT 1963

Illus. 86. Using a screw-driver.

SIZES OF BITS OR DRILLS TO BORE HOLES FOR WOOD SCREWS

NUMBER OF SCREW	1	2	3	4	5	6	7	8	9	10	12	14	16	18
BODY DIAMETER OF SCREW	.073	.086	.099	.112	.125	.138	.151	.164	.177	.190	.216	.242	.268	.294
FIRST HOLE — TWIST DRILL SIZE	5/64	3/32	3/32	7/64	1/8	9/64	5/32	11/64	11/64	3/16	7/32	1/4	17/64	19/64
FIRST HOLE — AUGER BIT NUMBER					2	2	3	3	3	3	4	4	5	6
SECOND HOLE — TWIST DRILL SIZE	1/16	5/64	3/32	7/64	1/8	9/64	5/32	11/64	3/16	7/32	1/4	9/32	5/16	21/64
SECOND HOLE — AUGER BIT NUMBER							3	3	3	3	4	4	5	6

EXACT SIZES CANNOT BE GIVEN FOR THE HOLES FOR WOOD SCREWS. THE ABOVE ARE APPROXIMATELY RIGHT FOR AVERAGE NEEDS. VARIATIONS IN HARD AND SOFT WOOD, MOISTURE CONTENT AND SNUG OR LOOSE FITS, IF DESIRED, SHOULD BE CONSIDERED. NUMBER AND LETTER SIZES OF DRILLS ARE AVAILABLE, IF MORE EXACT SIZES ARE WANTED. A TRIAL FIT IN SCRAP WOOD IS PRACTICAL sizes (Illus. 87). Hand drills and bit braces can also be fitted with screw-driver bits for those of you who don't wish to invest in cordless or other power screwdrivers. These manual tools are helpful for increasing speed and preventing the kinds of marks a power screwdriver makes when driving slotted screws (Illus. 86).

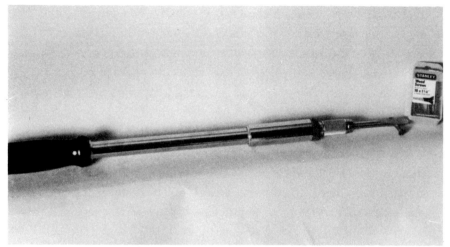

Illus. 87. A heavy-duty model Yankee ratcheting screwdriver.

MEASURING TOOLS

In general, measuring tools are close to the top on any list of carpentry tools. It is quite possible to build successfully without buying the most sophisticated types of rules, tapes, levels, and so on, although you will probably want to use fairly current materials that are standardized.

For straight measurement, the old-fashioned folding rule is still your best bet (Illus. 88, 89). It is available in 6-foot and 8-foot models. The good ones

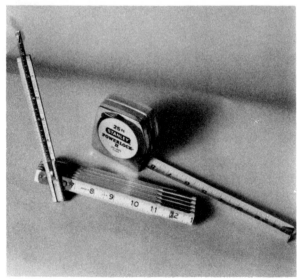

Illus. 88. Folding rule is in the foreground, and a 25-foot tape measure is in the back.

Illus. 89. Tilt both tapes and rules so the markings are close to the board to provide the most accurate measure-ments.

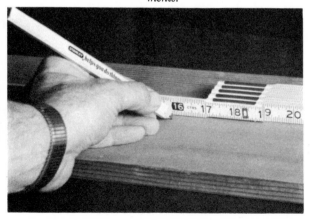

have brass-bound hinges, and the best models have a brass insert for extending measurements another 6 inches or for measuring hole depth. Most are made of wood and painted yellow with black markings, though you may find a few of fibreglass. I once had an aluminum one. It never broke, but within a couple of months it bent so much I couldn't rely on it.

Measuring tapes are a different story entirely. You can get these in lengths over 150 feet if you wish to spend the money. In most cases, a 12-foot or 16-foot tape is more than sufficient, while for fence work you may find a 50-foot tape is best. Again, types vary, but even the 50-foot tapes today are made with spring-powered rewind. For tapes up to 30-feet or so in length, you should look for a 1-inch-wide blade. Tapes longer than that are almost always narrower to reduce size and weight. Markings should be clear and consistent, and the case should be sturdy. If the tape has a rewind mechanism, be sure it also has some sort of brake. Otherwise the last foot or so that enters the case hard on retraction (which is actually the first foot of tape) snaps off and requires the purchase of a whole new tape or a new cartridge.

Though you'll seldom need to make fence panels level (stepped panels running down the side of a hill are an exception), a good level is an essential tool (Illus. 90) for making the posts as vertical as possible to the ground, so that other parts fit correctly. In general, a 2-foot-long level will provide a good indication of verticality (plumb) for all but the roughest posts. However, if buying too many special tools is becoming too expensive, purchase a good quality torpedo level and use that for all such work (Illus. 91).

Illus. 90. Combination square, wood level, metal level. Both levels are 2-feet long.

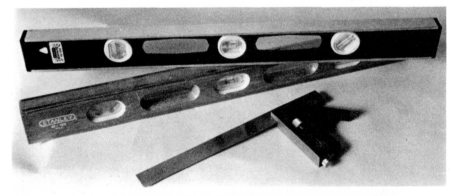

Illus. 91. A line level (foreground) and a torpedo level.

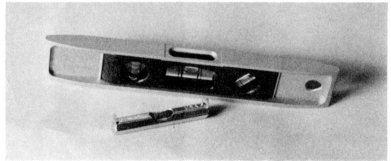

One other type of level may prove handy in running fence line layouts. It is the line level (Illus. 91), which is a small tool about 3 inches long with a single bubble element. Designed to hook over mason's cord that has been stretched taut, it is used for sighting lines on long fence runs and for running levels for any purpose over an extensive length of ground.

Squares of three types may prove helpful during fence construction. You will find that the combination square will be most useful. It has a blade that slips through the handle, providing either a 90° measure or a 45° measure. It also has a level bubble, which should be ignored because squares take too much battering for that bubble to stay accurate for long. A try square (Illus. 92) is similar to a combination square, but the blade is attached to the

Illus. 92. Try square.

handle at a permanent 90° angle. It is sturdier, but provides a much shorter, thus less accurate, 45° measure to make up for longer term accuracy at 90°. A carpenter's, or framing, square (Illus. 93) has so many uses it is nearly

Illus. 93. A carpenter's pencil rests on a carpenter's, or framing, square, with stair gauges in place. A marking gauge rests on the sliding T bevel at center, and a 16-foot tape is at center left.

impossible to describe them all. From the simple determination of square corners on small objects to the layout of rafters, stairs, and other complex angles, this tool is an essential. You may or may not require one for work on fences, but if you want to build stiles (steps over fences), you'll almost certainly need a framing square.

Marking tools, which might be categorized with measuring tools, include the carpenter's pencil. In the case of fencing, most marking can be done with its broad, easily sharpened lead, or a scribe. For long rip cuts, a marking gauge is handy, too, while for transferring angles from one point to another, a sliding T bevel is needed.

DIGGING TOOLS

Most of us consider ourselves familiar with shovels, though our range is sketchy compared to the items shown in a single company's catalog. For fence construction a shovel with a D handle and a pointed blade will almost always be sufficient. You will probably do most digging with a posthole digger and clean up and refill the postholes with a shovel. It still makes sense to get a good quality shovel.

Posthole diggers (Illus. 67, page 67) are nothing but elongated clamshells with long handles. The blades are made of steel, with a span of about one-half foot at rest. (This may vary upwards by 3 to 4 inches.) The handles are of ash or hickory (the stronger hickory is preferred). You pick the spot to start digging and slam the blades into the ground. Then move the handles apart, closing the blades around the earth. Lift, move the handles together to dump the dirt, and repeat (and remember to keep your hands away from the inner parts of the handles when dumping dirt to avoid hurting your knuckles).

Buy a good quality posthole digger because the price difference between the worst and best is negligible. There are several varieties available, and the light-duty models are good only in sandy ground. If you live in an area with heavy clay soil, only the heaviest posthole digger will work, and even then, after just a few holes, you'll be praying for a powered auger.

Powered posthole augers are rentable. Be sure that the model you rent includes instructions, either written ones from the manufacturer or verbal ones from the dealer. Essentially, it is composed of a powered drill bit, or auger bit, that moves down into the dirt, moving the discarded earth up its coil just as a drill bit would. Powered augers are available in one- and two-man models to suit your situation. Do not even consider the various hand-powered posthole augers available.

If you're lucky enough to have a tractor with a power take-off (PTO), then use the special type of posthole digger that attaches to it. These provide the fastest and easiest posthole digging for most people, but they are also the most expensive.

Any other tools you might need will be discussed as their use arises, including stretchers for various kinds of wire fences, fencing pliers (Illus. 94), and so on (Illus. 95).

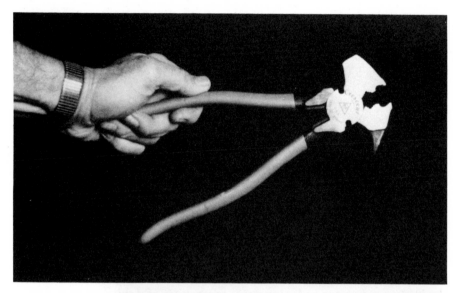

Illus. 94. Top-of-the-line Crescent fencing pliers, an exceptionally handy tool for wire fencing.

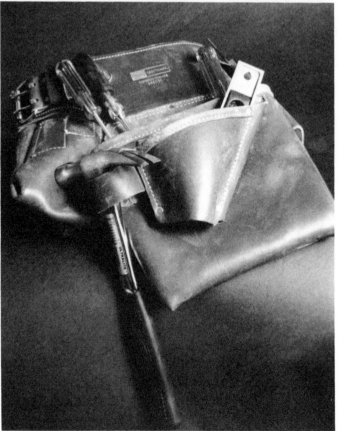

Illus. 95. An apron, like this Sears Craftsman tool apron, is indispensable for fence builders. This model has enough pockets and gadget hooks to hold every hand tool you need, so that once you leave your house in the morning, you won't have to hike back for special tools all day.

9 • Planning and Layout

After determining your proposed fence's function, look over your property, check the local codes, and make sure you know *where* the fence is going to go, so you can order the proper amount and type of materials.

Making a plan is somewhat tedious but will probably save you money in the long run. I've seen any number of fences go up quite well without one, but the builders had a couple of things going for them you may not. They had been erecting fences for twenty or more years, and the fences were used to outline pastures and hay fields, so tolerances were quite liberal. If a line of postholes was off as much as 6 feet one way or the other, it made no difference because property lines weren't involved and the prices for locally cut locust posts and barbed wire were low.

In suburban areas, and with more complex fencing styles, a plan and on-site layout are essential.

CHECKING BOUNDARIES

If you want a fence to be on or near one of your property lines (Illus. 96) you need to check the property to ascertain its limits. It's not a good idea to build fences on someone else's property, nor is it a good idea to move boundary fences any farther back onto your own property than building code setbacks demand (if they demand any at all).

Unfortunately, property lines are seldom readily visible. And in some suburban and many rural areas they are only vaguely described in deeds and other documents. Often such descriptions read as follows: "from the white oak at the northeast corner, step off 200 feet directly south . . ." Back in 1823, when that white oak was about 18 inches in diameter, such a description and a compass were all you needed. Even assuming the tree made it through the ensuing 160 or so years, you'd be working with a plant some 4 to 5 feet in diameter, which would significantly change the plot's

Illus. 96. This post-and-rail boundary fence is made of chestnut. Note that at any point a gate can be made by simply removing the rails from one section.

limits. Most likely, the tree would have died, or like the red oak on my front lawn, would have fallen into a number of sections during a windstorm.

If your land hasn't been professionally surveyed and staked, you probably will have no choice but to hire a professional to do the job for you. If it has been surveyed in the past, the dimensions and corner locations should be marked on the lot plat, which is usually filed in the country, town, or city courthouse. Stakes may be buried and hard to locate. In upstate New York some years ago, I found stakes that had been placed in an old loose stone wall and then covered with more stones. Usually, the materials hiding the stakes are brush or a few inches of dirt. Modern stakes are made of metal, and finding one gives you a starting point from which you can go on to find the others. If you know your stakes are made of metal, try finding them with a magnetic stud finder. Use a metal detector if that doesn't work. By following the lot plat you should be able to locate the other markers.

If the markers have disappeared, you can take a 12-ounce chalk bottle, which contains powdered chalk like that used in a chalk line. Tie a piece of mason's cord to the bottle neck and to the one known marker, making sure the distance between the bottle tip and the marker is the exact distance of one of the lost markers. Swing the chalk bottle in an arc in the general direction of the lost marker and carefully check along the arc and about 6 to 12 inches to each side. If the marker is still there, you should find it. Once that marker is found, you can repeat the procedure to find the remaining two if they're needed in your layout.

In addition to finding boundary markers, the largest problem in setting a fence line is keeping the line straight as it crests a rise and disappears from view. If you stand with one foot touching, or stand a specified distance from, a pair of boundary markers, you can proceed with no problem. But if you can't see from one end to the other end, you'll need to gather up a few friends and some straight poles. Usually, the job requires at least four people, though in a pinch you might get by with three.

Two people (*A* and *D*), one at the starting stake and one at the end point, will be out of sight of each other. They should be holding moderately tall (at least 6-feet high) straight poles. In between, two other people (*B* and *C*) should stand as directly in line as a rapid sighting makes possible. The latter two helpers (*B* and *C*) each need an 8-foot or taller pole. Now, *A* and *B* should be in sight of each other, and *C* and *D* should be in sight of each other. Now, *B* and *C* adjust their stakes until they are in a straight line. Next, repeat the process to the next point. The four points should now be in a straight line and stakes can be driven. Run mason's cord from stake to stake to maintain that line. See Illus. 97 for an easy method of determining corners and making them square.

Illus. 97. Setting boundary markers and end posts. To ensure perfect corners set posts a few feet beyond the stake and insert a nail in each. Then tie cord to the nail and stretch between posts so that the two cord pieces intersect at the boundary stake. After your selection of wood, the most important part of construction in terms of durability is the correct setting of posts to their appropriate depths.

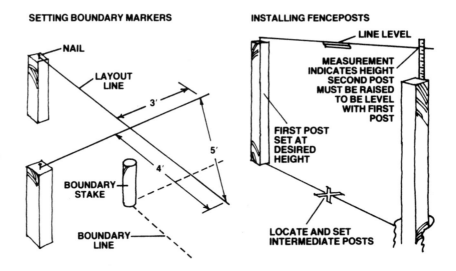

SETTING BOUNDARY MARKERS

NAIL

LAYOUT LINE

3'

5'

4'

BOUNDARY STAKE

BOUNDARY LINE

INSTALLING FENCEPOSTS

LINE LEVEL

MEASUREMENT INDICATES HEIGHT SECOND POST MUST BE RAISED TO BE LEVEL WITH FIRST POST

FIRST POST SET AT DESIRED HEIGHT

LOCATE AND SET INTERMEDIATE POSTS

Also be sure to mark entry points with stakes. The determination of intermediate points can start from any corner, but if appearance is important, start with the most visible corner. Begin by making sure all corners are staked properly and entryways are roughly marked. Run cotton mason's cord tightly between the stakes in such a way that the posts can be placed inside the cord. The outside edge of the posts should barely touch the inside edge of the cord.

Using chalk, mark on the twine the exact spot where each posthole should be dug (Illus. 98). Arrange the posts according to their correct size.

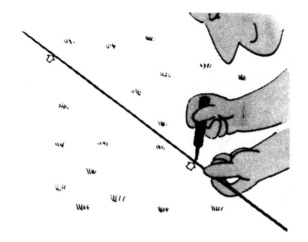

Illus. 98. Marking a fence line. The procedure is virtually the same for all fence types.

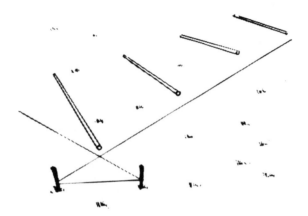

Illus. 99. Stretching the cord along the line.

Line posts are the smallest in diameter, while corner and gateposts should be about 25 percent larger (Illus. 99).

Make a story pole (from scrap wood) that is as long as one section of fence. Fence sections, or panels, will usually be 8, 10, or 12 feet long. Occasionally they measure 16 feet. For privacy screens and windbreaks, the sections may be only 4 feet long to offer the full 8-foot height of a piece of plywood, but even then 8-foot lengths are more common.

Cut several foot-long sharpened stakes, and starting at the main corner, drive one into the ground where each fence post will ultimately be inserted, using the story pole along the strung mason's cord (from corner stake to corner stake) to set section lengths.

Adjust locations for gates, gateposts, special fence sections, and so on at this time, using the story pole. It is easier to shift a gatepost a foot or two in one direction or another than it is to build a gate in an odd size. So adjust the fence section instead of the gate size.

Once all post locations are staked, you can determine the materials needed for the job almost exactly, if you haven't already made your estimates.

Most fence styles follow the slope of the ground, but some are stepped to accommodate a hillside. Each section top is level, but each section rises with the incline (Illus. 100). A picket fence looks best if laid out along a fairly flat section so the top is kept level. Of course, when the ground slants too abruptly, you may wish to simply change the design of the pickets, so the fence runs along the ground contour instead of level. One solution is to make concave and convex tops over a fairly large section of fence.

Illus. 100. Here are several solutions for constructing a fence on a hillside. Remember, though, much depends on the purpose of the fence.

Adjust central fence sections to make up for off readings at end sections. In other words, if your fence consists of 8-foot panels, and the total length of one side is 83 feet, don't make one end panel 11 feet long. Erect ten 8-foot panels and slip the remaining 3 feet in along the way, in units less than one foot, which should make the longer panels hardly noticeable. Most wood fencing, even the factory-cut kind, usually includes a few inches of slack in each section.

With all this in mind, you can make a far more accurate estimate of how much you will need than by running around the perimeter of your land with a tape measure and saying, "Well, we need 1,000 feet of rail for here, and about forty posts, with four of those corner posts and four gateposts." With accurate measurements, you'll know you need forty-six or thirty-eight or nine posts, and 1450 feet of rail in 10-foot or 8-foot or 12-foot lengths, and so on. It may sound like a large investment of time to save a few hours during construction and a few dollars on materials. But if you check the cost of quality construction materials for almost any form of fencing, you'll quickly find that planning is worth it.

Once you know the amount of material required, you can determine what type to use and the order in which it should be delivered as well as the probable tools, nails, and staples needed for the work to come.

10 ◆ Erecting Fences

So now, we can come down to it—the real work, the digging and pounding and pulling and toting and bruised fingers and sore toes and banged shins. If you don't expect at least some physical discomfort, you should read only the first parts of this book and then hire someone else to install your fence. I know of no one who has survived the construction of a large fence without at least some muscle soreness, a few splinters, and some bruises. It can be heavy work, and the posthole digging can be very nasty if you work in clay ground. Not too long ago, I needed only five 4-foot-deep postholes, so I couldn't justify the expense of hiring a farmer for 30 minutes with his PTO posthole digger, nor could I justify renting a one- or two-man power auger. As a result, I had to dig the holes with a manual posthole digger.

You can believe I waited a full week to insert the posts after digging the holes. I was so sick of the job I didn't even want to *look* at it for that length of time.

Generally, though, once the fence line is laid out and the posthole positions marked, the job goes relatively quickly, almost surprisingly so for simpler fence forms (board, simple wire mesh, wire strands).

INSTALLING WOODEN-POST FENCES

We'll assume by now you've got your general fence boundaries lined out with mason's cord. Mason's cord is best because it is made of tightly woven cotton that stretches only a little. Nylon or some other synthetic cord might be handier, but if the work must sit more than a few hours, the nylon will stretch, producing a sag and possible problems with correct alignment and height. Set boundary markers if the fence is to be on a boundary. (See Illus. 96, page 89.) Make certain, though, that the fence will not extend even inches onto a neighbor's property or, probably far worse, onto public property. You might want to talk to your neighbor to confirm the boundary's locations. But talking to a bureaucracy about public property will probably require a lawyer and lots of cash.

To be sure the corners are perfectly square, use the 3-4-5-foot method (Illus. 97, page 90) to make sure you've got a right angle, then place the first and last pole in a line. Next, determine as precisely as possible the position for intermediate posts (you may wish to postpone this job until after the line-end posts are set).

Once you decide where the posts should be installed, then dig the postholes. If the soil is easy to work, use the basic hand posthole digger. Otherwise, rent a tractor-driven (PTO) digger or a gas-powered one- or two-man auger. As a rule of thumb, dig the postholes one third the length of the post. In other words, for a 4-foot-high fence, you need 6-foot-long posts and 2-foot-deep holes. I prefer line-end (termination) posts to be 25 percent larger than the regular line posts. This isn't always practical: if you're working with the basic 4″ × 4″ post, it's usually simpler to go up 50 percent to 6″ × 6″. Use the same size increase for *all* gateposts as a minimum. You may well need a full 50 percent larger post for heavy or wide gates.

Once the postholes are dug, you can start setting posts (Illus. 101), taking

Illus. 101. Setting posts.

into consideration your style of fence and the soil and weather conditions in your area. If you live around Tucson, Arizona, for example, a simple hole backfilled with its own sandy dirt is sufficient for normal strength. Undersurface bracing or the addition of concrete in the hole may be added for strength, but usually no special drainage precautions are required.

In areas with clay soils (almost always those where I've had to build fences), your fence will last longer if you provide drainage (Illus. 102). Even woods such as redwood, cedar, cypress, or pressure-treated woods need

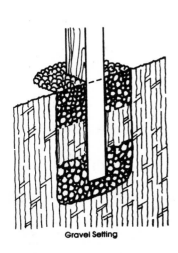

Gravel Setting

Cross Cleat Setting for Gate Posts

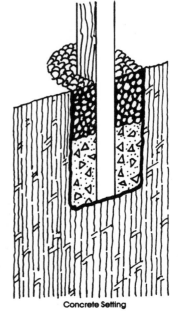

Concrete Setting

Illus. 102. Methods of making sure the posts stay put for a long, long time.

Secure posts

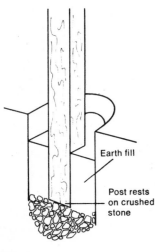

Earth fill

Post rests on crushed stone

protection in certain soils. First, dig the hole at least 6 inches deeper than the post will be set. Then fill 5 inches of that space with loose, medium-size gravel and place a flat rock on the top. Then insert the post and replace the soil. Again, undersurface bracing or concrete may be used to add strength to the post setting if necessary, but they will greatly increase both installation time and expense.

To dig postholes, start with the digger handles held apart a bit. This not only helps protect your hands—which should be above and below, not directly opposite on, the handles—but also takes a smaller bite of dirt at the surface where you're getting an indication of the difficulty of digging, for one thing, and where you're probably working your way through a layer of sod for another. Close up the handles and take bigger bites as you go down, if the ground allows. If not, continue with small bites. Place a piece of masking or duct tape on one or both handles to indicate proper depth so that you don't have to constantly measure the depth. Don't stripe the handles with paint or ink unless you expect every posthole to go to the

Illus. A1. A small redwood overhead creates a shady corner and echoes a trellis-fence theme.

Illus. A2. Construction grades of redwood in board and trellis combination.

A

Illus. B1. This redwood fence separates pool and entry court. Rugged, knot-textured redwood Garden grades have natural beauty and outstanding weatherability.

Illus. B2. This post-board-and-rail fence of Clear-grade redwood encloses a corner-lot back yard and screens out street sights and sounds. Spacing of the boards can be varied to achieve the desired amount of air flow and privacy.

Illus. B3. A simple post-and-rail redwood fence makes an attractive boundary marker.

B

Illus. C1. The solid redwood fence behind this fibreglass spa is combined with airy, diagonal redwood lath screen fencing.

Illus. C2. This decorative redwood fence with trellis provides wind protection and rustic, natural beauty.

C

Illus. D1. Redwood fencing is personalized with a bench and deck to create a place for casual outdoor entertaining.

Illus. D2. The California Redwood Association calls this a view fence. The panels are framed in 2-by material to break up the lines of a pretty standard vertical board fence . . . you might otherwise feel hemmed in by the fence.

D

same depth—that is, every posthole you dig until the paint or ink wears off. As you approach final hole depth, widen the hole base, leaving the top nearly the original size (two or three times the diameter of the post being planted) (Table 6, page 124). The wider base makes room for more gravel and increases drainage, but it is most important if you're attaching boards or rods for below-surface post supports (Illus. 102).

Once the postholes are dug, set the posts near them and, finally, loosely in them. If the fence is to be made of boards that have been cut on site, or made of wire, the posts can now be planted and tamped in place. A regular steel tamper isn't really necessary. I tend to use an old piece of 2″ × 4″ about 4 to 5 feet long.

If you erect a post-and-rail fence, set the posts firmly at the corners but leave the rest of them moderately loose all around the enclosure (except at gates). The reason is simple: rails are usually a few inches longer than the spacing between posts, and you'll have to jiggle the posts to get rails in on both sides. Once all rails are in place for a section, take your level and plumb the posts.

For other fences, plumb the posts as you erect them. Wire fences with wooden posts usually require bracing of corner panels, or sections, and often need some form of bracing in intermediate sections if the fence is long. The reason this is needed for a wire fence and not for a board fence is simple: boards are their own braces, but wire, which is flexible and easier to install, is less likely to stiffen the fence.

Most strand wire and wire mesh placed on wood posts are stapled into place with fence staples and a good 16- or 20-ounce carpenter's hammer. If none is around, use your fencing pliers, which will have at least a small nailing face. The hammer is preferable for nailing, and the fencing pliers serve as a general tool, enabling you to stretch, cut, staple, or unstaple wire, with the emphasis on cutting and stretching (over short distances) (Illus. 103).

Illus. 103. Fence pliers.

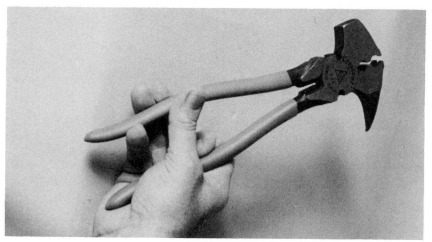

INSTALLING METAL-POST FENCES

You have several options for installing the round metal posts. They can be inserted into concrete that has been poured into a posthole. Some companies consider this method messy and time consuming. It does take longer and requires more clean-up time (Illus. 104). If you use an anchoring device and drive the posts into the ground, you can save time in digging and in mixing the concrete (Illus. 105). Unfortunately, soft sand and areas that contain many small rocks make such driving almost impossible.

Illus. 104. Concrete post-setting is messy but sometimes is best.

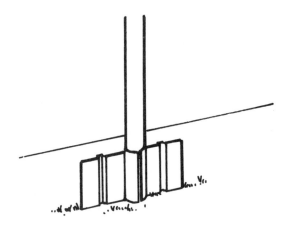

Illus. 105. Anchoring device enables posts to be driven in instead of dug in, and they hold well.

Illus. 106. Begin the installation with the corner and end posts.

Once the posts are in and plumb (Illus. 106), you can install the mesh fabric. To make sure the posts will accommodate the fabric, mark the base of the posts the same height as your chain-link fabric, minus 2 inches. Then drive in these line posts to that mark. Mark the larger posts for gates and

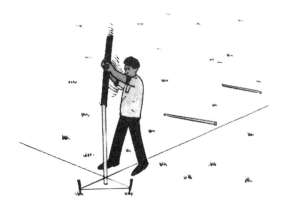

corners 3 inches longer than the fence fabric is high and set them to that mark.

Chain-link material should be attached to posts whose centers are no farther apart than 10 feet. It's best to even things out when possible: that is, a 45-foot-long fence would require posts set 9 feet apart (pages 105–106).

Position the corner posts and end posts so they just touch your string line (Fig. 107). If you're using a mechanical driver, lift it and let it fall until the post is driven down to its mark. Check verticality about every other blow.

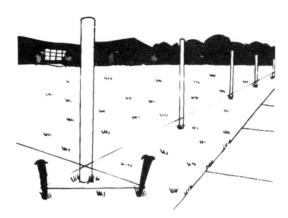

Illus. 107. Keep posts plumb and lined against the twine.

Driving posts to their marks will make sure your fence follows land contours correctly. Line posts are set in the same manner, again aligned with the edge of the twine. Before driving any post all the way in, check the top to make sure damage from the driver won't make fitting the cap impossible. Slight dings can be filed off, but sections with major damage will have to be cut off from the 2-inch margin you have provided.

Now install the fittings on corner and end posts, 1 foot apart with the flat side facing out. You can then add rail end bands and cups and tap the post caps into place. Place loop caps on the line posts, flat side facing the outside of the fence. The top rails run through the loop caps and are joined to make a single, continuous railing (Illus. 108–110).

Illus. 108. Installing fittings.

Illus. 109. Adding rail end bands and caps.

Illus. 110. Post with fittings installed.

Top rails are cut to fit snugly into end and corner posts. This job needs care to prevent the post from being pulled inward when the fabric is stretched (Illus. 111).

After tightening the end rail band, you now have all the framework in place. Unroll the chain-link fabric along the outside of the frame if there is enough space (Illus. 112). If not, unroll it from an upright position. The

Illus. 111. Installing the top rail.

Illus. 112. Unroll the fabric along the fence line.

fabric may be separated along the linked strands or joined through the linking of strands as if it were really a chain.

Slip a tension bar through the end of the fabric and position it on the post tension bands (Illus. 113). Then tighten the bands. Go along the fence and loosely fasten the fabric to the top rail with the tie wires that have been provided. Install a second tension bar about 9 feet from a corner or end post at the far end of the line, and attach the fabric stretcher to it (Illus. 114,

Illus. 113. Slip fabric into tension band and then tighten the band.

Illus. 114. Set second tension band 9' or so from the line end.

115). Taking up slack slowly, you'll soon see if there is so much slack that you will have to reposition the tension bar. If so, do it. Shake the fabric, lining up the diamonds, and give the stretcher another turn or two, getting the fabric extra tight (Illus. 116).

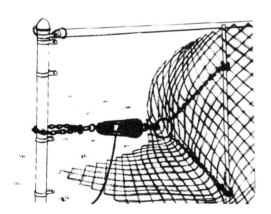

Illus. 115. Attach fabric stretcher.

Illus. 116. Shake and stretch chain-link fabric at least once after first stretching.

Hold the position while you tighten this set of tension bands, just as you did the ones at the beginning of the fence. Properly installed, the fabric will be tight, but with just a little flop in it.

There are a wide variety of gates and other accessories for wire fences, which are all factory made. It's generally best to use those made for your brand of fence so that problems don't arise later.

HILLSIDE FENCES

Building a fence on a hillside tends to present the most complex fencing problems, but there are a variety of solutions, as you can see in Illus. 117. If the slope isn't clifflike, you can usually follow the ground contours, just as you would with fencing on relatively level ground. For sections that are intermittently steep and not-so-steep, you could make a sharp tilt (A) while stacking boards (B and C) works on slight slopes. Stepped fencing works quite well on steep slopes but only with solid boards, louvers, and panels. It's virtually useless with post-and-rail, standard board, and all forms of wire fence.

Illus. 117. Solutions for building a fence on a hillside.

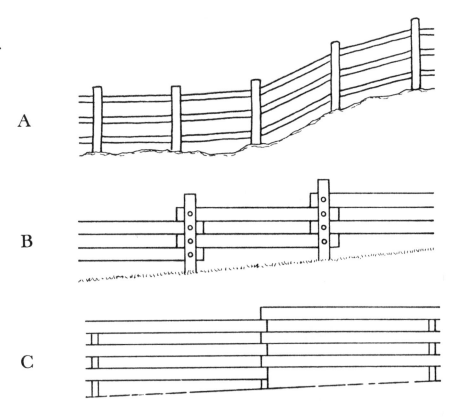

A

B

C

Fence style has been covered from place to place throughout and is a matter of individual choice. Simply give careful consideration to the choice of style versus the cost, final appearance, and the amount of work you'll need to do. Picket fences, for example, are lovely but too laborious for enclosing more than about 1/4 acre. Horizontal pickets, however, might be easier. They are nothing more than boards with one or both ends cut to a slanted design. They produce what is sometimes called a shaped-end fence, and you design the ends to suit your taste. Louvered fences present the same problems. There's a lot of work involved, so the fence works best over small areas.

JOINTS

Of the various joints needed to form a fence, only one is essential—the simple butt joint. For fancier fencing and special problems, for a railing around a deck, and for greater strength or decorative effect, use a variety of joints. The names vary a bit from those generally used in woodworking. They are named more for their position in the fence than for their style. Thus as Illus. 118 shows, an overlapping joint, where a top rail rests on a post, is nothing more than a butt joint. (See also Illus. 47.) Because it's placed on top of the post, it overlaps. Why a bias mitre joint is called a bias mitre joint rather than an overlapping mitre joint, I can't tell you: mitres are bias cuts by definition, so the name is redundant but used extensively.

Top rails and bottom rails usually require fancy joints and possibly fancy fasteners. Bottom rails in particular may require toe-nail, block, or metal-angle joints (Illus. 119).

Illus. 118. Fence joints. Almost all of these joints are easy to form, but you should use the simplest and easiest joints when building a long fence, so you save time and energy.

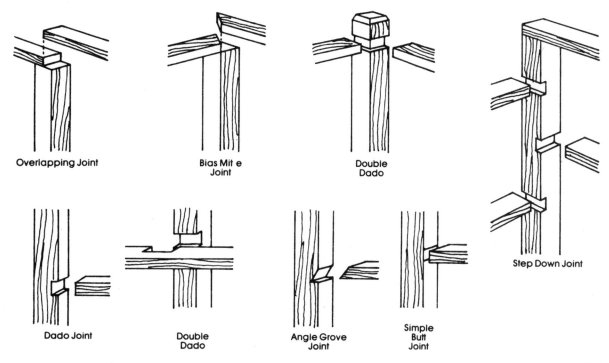

Overlapping Joint

Bias Mit e Joint

Double Dado

Step Down Joint

Dado Joint

Double Dado

Angle Grove Joint

Simple Butt Joint

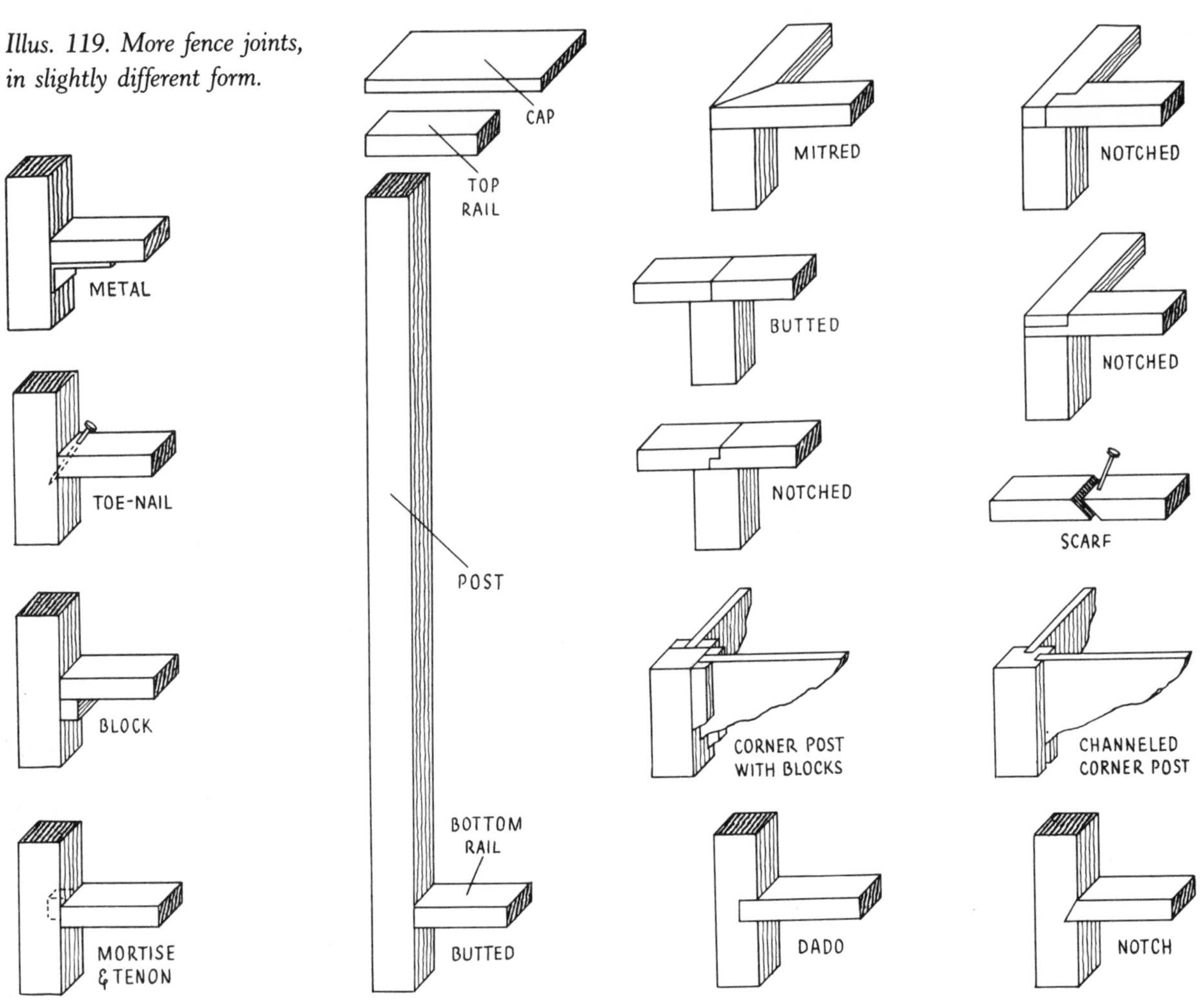

Illus. 119. More fence joints, in slightly different form.

METAL

TOE-NAIL

BLOCK

MORTISE & TENON

CAP

TOP RAIL

POST

BOTTOM RAIL

BUTTED

MITRED

BUTTED

NOTCHED

CORNER POST WITH BLOCKS

DADO

NOTCHED

NOTCHED

SCARF

CHANNELED CORNER POST

NOTCH

POST CAPS

All wooden fence posts need to be cut at a 15° angle (minimum) or to be capped with wood, metal, or other material so that water can easily run off the surface. This will prevent water from seeping into the post and protect it from rot and expansion (from freezing).

And remember, hardware must be at least weather resistant. Use hot-dipped galvanized nails, angles, and other metal bits or substitute those made of aluminum. This choice of weather-resistant fasteners is especially important if you plan to let the fence weather naturally. Regular nails will rust and stain the fence badly, drastically reducing its attractiveness.

Whether or not you apply a finish to a fence is a personal preference. My feeling is that the use of particularly durable wood at the outset precludes any need for a finish on most fences. Let them weather to a soft, natural grey, and they'll look better (with far less work) than any fence painted every twelve or fifteen years and then left to peel (Illus. 120). The probable exception is the picket fence surrounding a house. Such a fence is usually painted the same color as the trim of the house, though a basic white is also very popular. When you plan to erect a fence that needs to be painted, you should still use weather-resistant fasteners but consider a less durable grade of wood. It will save money and last about as long as durable wood *if* the paint or stain is renewed.

Illus. 120. Redwood fence with Lucite lights in the panels.

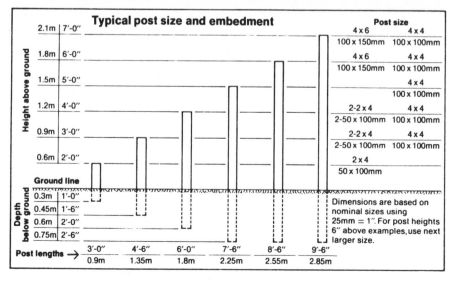

Typical post size and embedment

Height above ground		Post size	
		4 x 6	4 x 4
2.1m	7'-0"	100 x 150mm	100 x 100mm
		4 x 6	4 x 4
1.8m	6'-0"	100 x 150mm	100 x 100mm
			4 x 4
1.5m	5'-0"		100 x 100mm
		2-2 x 4	4 x 4
1.2m	4'-0"	2-50 x 100mm	100 x 100mm
		2-2 x 4	4 x 4
0.9m	3'-0"	2-50 x 100mm	100 x 100mm
		2 x 4	
0.6m	2'-0"	50 x 100mm	

Ground line

Depth below ground

0.3m	1'-0"	Dimensions are based on nominal sizes using 25mm = 1". For post heights 6" above examples, use next larger size.
0.45m	1'-6"	
0.6m	2'-0"	
0.75m	2'-6"	

Post lengths →

3'-0"	4'-6"	6'-0"	7'-6"	8'-6"	9'-6"
0.9m	1.35m	1.8m	2.25m	2.55m	2.85m

LINE-POST SPACING

—Measure the actual distance between any two end, corner, or gate posts.
—Find this distance under Space on the table.
—The dimension indicates the interval that should be used between line posts.

Space	Set Posts Apart	Space	Set Posts Apart	Space	Set Posts Apart	Space	Set Posts Apart	Space	Set Posts Apart	Space	Set Posts Apart
30 ft.	10 ft.	64 ft.	9 ft.	97 ft.	9 ft. 7 in.	48 ft.	9 ft. 7 in.	81 ft.	9 ft.	114 ft.	9 ft. 6 in.
31 ft.	7 ft. 9 in.	65 ft.	9 ft. 3 in.	98 ft.	9 ft. 8 in.	49 ft.	9 ft. 9 in.	82 ft.	9 ft. 1 in.	115 ft.	9 ft. 7 in.
32 ft.	8 ft.	66 ft.	9 ft. 5 in.	99 ft.	9 ft. 9 in.	50 ft.	10 ft.	83 ft.	9 ft. 3 in.	116 ft.	9 ft. 8 in.
33 ft.	8 ft. 3 in.	67 ft.	9 ft. 7 in.	100 ft.	10 ft.	51 ft.	8 ft. 6 in.	84 ft.	9 ft. 4 in.	117 ft.	9 ft. 9 in.
34 ft.	8 ft. 6 in.	68 ft.	9 ft. 8 in.	101 ft.	9 ft. 2 in.	52 ft.	8 ft. 8 in.	85 ft.	9 ft. 6 in.	118 ft.	9 ft. 10 in.
35 ft.	8 ft. 9 in.	69 ft.	9 ft. 10 in.	102 ft.	9 ft. 3 in.	53 ft.	8 ft. 10 in.	86 ft.	9 ft. 7 in.	119 ft.	9 ft. 10 in.
36 ft.	9 ft.	70 ft.	10 ft.	103 ft.	9 ft. 4 in.	54 ft.	9 ft.	87 ft.	9 ft. 8 in.	120 ft.	10 ft.
37 ft.	9 ft. 3 in.	71 ft.	8 ft. 9 in.	104 ft.	9 ft. 5 in.	55 ft.	8 ft. 2 in.	88 ft.	9 ft. 9 in.	121 ft.	9 ft. 3 in.
38 ft.	9 ft. 6 in.	72 ft.	9 ft.	105 ft.	9 ft. 6 in.	56 ft.	9 ft. 4 in.	89 ft.	9 ft. 10 in.	122 ft.	9 ft. 4 in.
40 ft.	10 ft.	73 ft.	9 ft. 2 in.	106 ft.	9 ft. 7 in.	57 ft.	9 ft. 6 in.	90 ft.	10 ft.	123 ft.	9 ft. 5 in.
41 ft.	8 ft. 2 in.	74 ft.	9 ft. 3 in.	107 ft.	9 ft. 8 in.	58 ft.	9 ft. 8 in.	91 ft.	9 ft. 2 in.	124 ft.	9 ft. 6 in.
42 ft.	8 ft. 5 in.	75 ft.	9 ft. 4 in.	108 ft.	9 ft. 9 in.	59 ft.	9 ft. 10 in.	92 ft.	9 ft. 2 in.	125 ft.	9 ft. 7 in.
43 ft.	8 ft. 6 in.	76 ft.	9 ft. 6 in.	109 ft.	9 ft. 10 in.	60 ft.	10 ft.	93 ft.	9 ft. 3 in.	126 ft.	9 ft. 8 in.
44 ft.	8 ft. 9 in.	77 ft.	9 ft. 7 in.	110 ft.	10 ft.	61 ft.	8 ft. 8 in.	94 ft.	9 ft. 5 in.	127 ft.	9 ft. 9 in.
45 ft.	9 ft.	78 ft.	9 ft. 9 in.	111 ft.	9 ft. 3 in.	62 ft.	8 ft. 1 in.	95 ft.	9 ft. 6 in.	128 ft.	9 ft. 10 in.
46 ft.	9 ft. 2 in.	79 ft.	9 ft. 10 in.	112 ft.	9 ft. 4 in.	63 ft.	9 ft.	96 ft.	9 ft. 7 in.	129 ft.	9 ft. 10 in.
47 ft.	9 ft. 5 in.	80 ft.	10 ft.	113 ft.	9 ft. 5 in.						

Illus. 121. This redwood lattice fence provides privacy for the redwood pavilion with Jacuzzi. The fence is constructed with vertical and horizontal redwood slats anchored to 4″ × 4″ redwood posts.

106

11 · Gates

Farmers like to argue about the most important part of any fence line, and sooner or later the subject of gates turns up. A fenced-off area isn't much good without some form of access, and there are only two ways to enter such an area without clambering over the fence: gates and stiles. Stiles are of far less importance because they are placed as stress relievers at points far away from gates; they're nothing more than stairs passing through the fence to enable you, me, and every goat in the country to get over the fence without straining the boards, posts, or wires. Gates, though, provide entrances (and exits) at particular spots for particular reasons.

Illus. 122. This heavy-duty screen was erected in wind-break style. Note the diagonal board used to brace the gate.

In addition to meeting requirements for access, gates must be sturdy enough to last a long time with little sign of wear and tear. Most don't last very long, and wear and tear show up promptly, the results of bad construction or poor design.

GATE PLANNING

Illus. 123. Trellis-shaded redwood fencing around a brick-paved entry/courtyard with built-in planters.

Probably thirty minutes of thought on structure will make a gate much more convenient to use and much more durable. First, make sure the gate is going to open wide enough to accommodate anything that will pass through it. If that one requirement is overlooked, you may be constructing a

useless item. If the gate is too small, road graders and trucks and wheelbarrows and garden carts will soon render the gate useless. If the gate is too large to build easily, you'll be tempted to buy inferior and fewer materials and build it hastily to save time. There are ways to save money on gate materials, but skimping isn't one. The first way to save money on gates is to install only as many as are, or will be, needed. Use stiles for other fence crossings. The second way is appropriate for wire fences: use what is known (whether accurately or not, I don't know) as a Texas gate. In a barbed-wire fence, a Texas gate is nothing more than a section of the barbed-wire strands, which are attached at the strand ends to a small pole, which then is attached to the main post with wire loops. These gates work well and require only as much time and as many materials to build as a section or panel of barbed-wire fence does. Be sure, though, to use smooth wire to make the attaching loops. In the South, most people make those loops out of barbed wire, which means they don't have to cart two types of wire around. But it also means that the barbed wire is painful for ungloved hands especially in cold weather when the iced-up loops are difficult to move anyway.

Gates for residential use generally fall into two categories: those for foot traffic and those for vehicles. Small gates (usually under 48 inches wide but never less than 32 inches wide) are appropriate for basic foot-traffic, while wider gates (8 feet and more, even in these days of peanut-sized cars, 10 feet is a far preferable width) are better for vehicles (Illus. 124). In general, an attractive gate follows the design of the fence, where possible (Illus. 125). (Flimsy fences, however, should not have flimsy gates. Like all fences, they

Illus. 124. Two gate styles, shown here, look entirely different but are built on exactly the same type of frame. This basic gate frame will serve for most styles of wooden fences. Use a double unit where a wider gate is required.

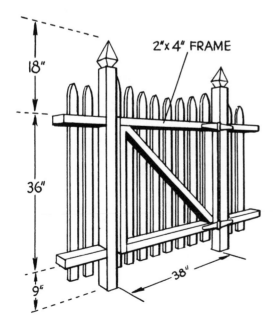

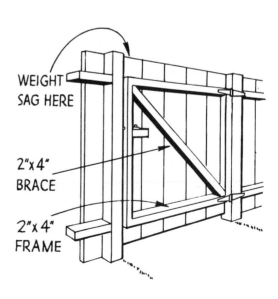

109

Illus. 125. A redwood gate
perfectly suited to its fence.

still require durable gates.) Wire fences for farms, on the other hand, may vary widely in their gate requirements.

All gate hardware must be of top quality and well protected from corrosion by a coating of paint, chrome, nickel, or zinc (galvanized). You can use aluminum hardware, but it is less practical for such items as hinges and latches where a hard surface is much more important than weight. The items shown in Illus. 126–128 are from a single maker, Stanley Hardware,

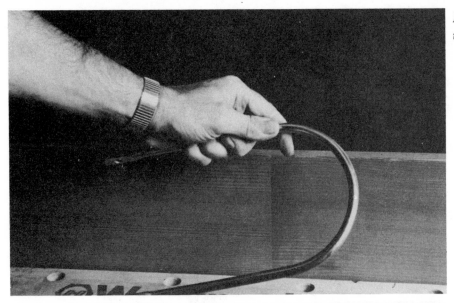

Illus. 126. Loop gate fastener.

Illus. 127. Extra heavy-duty gate spring.

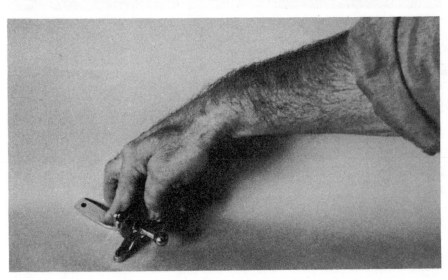

Illus. 128. Chromed gate latch is sturdy, operates easily, and lasts for years.

and do not represent even a small section of their line. The quality is excellent, which is why I chose them.

As Illus. 129 shows, simple latches may be made for board, picket, and other wooden fence styles, and Illus. 130 shows that even for walkway gates, cross bracing is often, if not always, needed. The wider the gate, the heavier the bracing needed.

Illus. 129. Simple homemade gate latch.

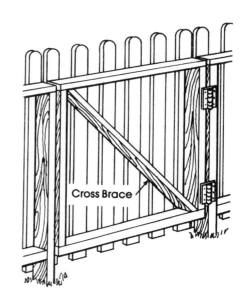

Cross Brace

Illus. 130. Hinges attached to the gate.

Illus. 131. Purchased sheet-metal gate.

In Illus. 131, 132, and 133, I've pictured a gate and some of the gate hardware on the farm where I currently live. The gate was manufactured of

Illus. 132. Screw-in hinge pin for sheet-metal gate.

Illus. 133. Welded-on hinge loop for sheet-metal gate.

galvanized sheet metal, while the hinge loop and the hinge pin are of heavier metal. Similar gates are available made of pipe, also galvanized, with sizes starting at 10 feet wide and going to about 16 feet wide. If it were my choice, I'd find a way to use two 10-foot gates before I'd erect a 16-foot model. First, each post would not have to carry as large a load. Second, each gate would weigh less, so it would last longer.

As Illus. 134 shows, gateposts are best set in concrete. This holds true for almost any gate. (Farmers, though, often bypass this step because of the cost and mess, and the extra 3 to 7 days they must wait for the concrete to cure.) This narrow gate has been carefully plumbed and levelled, and the same care must be applied to larger gates, obviously. Posts are temporarily held together with nailed-on struts until the concrete cures. (You should probably wait a full seven days, and I prefer ten. You can get away with three, but no less than that.) If the gate is metal, you can either leave it off if post setting is done with exacting care, or wire it in place instead of nailing it on through wood struts.

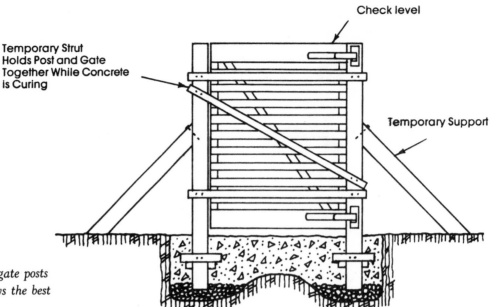

Check level

Temporary Strut
Holds Post and Gate
Together While Concrete
is Curing

Temporary Support

Illus. 134. Setting gate posts in concrete is always the best method.

Illus. 135. A gate anti-sag kit manufactured by Stanley Tools. This simple-to-use kit will provide extra support for gates that have already sagged or will help prevent sag in gates that are expected to get extremely heavy wear. The cable is placed on the diagonal and tightened with the turnbuckle. Cable is over 7 feet long, so one kit is sufficient for most single gates, and two kits are sufficient for most double gates, though you may wish to develop your own method for gates over 5 feet wide. It requires only cable and a turnbuckle that will accept that cable, plus cable end fasteners, which may be simply screws around which the cable is wound before the screws are tightened all the way.

Nonresidential fence gates—those on farms or ranches—are generally wider. Still, the fence will provide the basis for the gate design, with cross bracing added as required. You can buy special bracing kits, either for use at the outset or to repair gates that begin to sag. Such kits include galvanized cable, fasteners, and a small turnbuckle to facilitate future adjustments (Illus. 135). If you require a gate more than 12 feet wide, particularly for a board fence, then consider making it a double gate. The gate will last far longer and will be easier to erect. And it's not really all that much harder to open and close a two-part gate. In fact, just today I noticed a farm that has a quadruple gate. Apparently, the owner required (and got) a huge opening in the fence. Thus, he installed very large fence posts (at least 150 percent of

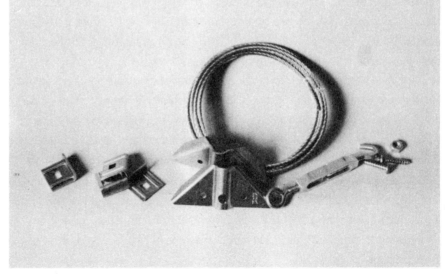

the line-post size). He then set a 10-foot section on each post, and, finally, attached an 8-foot section that folded back onto the 10-foot sections as the gate opened. Overall, the opening seems to be about 36 feet wide. (I'd like to be there some day to photograph whatever it is he drives through that monster opening, for farms in my area do not require the types of large equipment common in the Midwest.)

Gates, then, are not difficult. Make the diameter of the posts 25 percent larger (normally) than line posts and add 6 to 12 inches to their lengths. Set in concrete where possible or add below-surface supports if not. Accurately plumb all such posts so the gate latches will be easy to line up (and will stay lined up). Make sure you place a gate of the correct size nearest to where it will be needed (Illus. 136–138).

Illus. 136. A gateway in Arizona that has been erected around a sheet-metal gate.

Illus. 137. Detail of Illus. 136 gatepost top. Note the handmade brace.

Illus. 138. This homemade gate lock was made from steel tubing and concrete tie rod. You could also make hinges in the same manner.

Erecting dozens of gates, though, is obviously neither economical nor practical. Wire fences with Texas gates are something of an exception, and even that gate style tends to weaken a fence a bit. A stile might be a better solution. A stile is simply a set of stairs that goes through a wire or board fence. You don't have to keep riser and tread sizes within the recommended figures for home staircases. The idea is to get over a fence, not up a set of stairs. Thus, extend a 2″ × 10″ board that is (usually) 4 feet wide between each set of boards or strands of wire. Fit these treads to stringers made of other 2″ × 10″ boards, cut and attach them to provide the required number of steps to the stile so the last step is just under the top strand of wire or top fence board. The stile, of course, extends through the fence. Up one side, down the other; not a double flight of stairs, one up and one down, but a single flight rising to just below the top of the fence, and extending *through* the fence, so all that's needed is to turn and walk down the second side.

Don't use stiles if you are trying to keep goats or smart hogs in a field. It takes a goat about 17 nanoseconds to figure out how to get out, and a rather slow hog takes only 30 minutes to realize its trotters might make it over to greener pastures. (But if they don't and if the hog is large and fat, then all that bacon and ham gets hung up on the fence and lots of firewood—the remains of the stile—fall to the ground.)

For fences that cross streams choose another form of gate.

STORM GATES

Storm gates are relatively simple affairs most of the time. If a stream bed cuts though a fence line, sometimes you can build the fence across the stream with no problems. If the stream is wide or subject to flooding (and almost every narrow stream and most wide ones I've ever seen are subject to flooding) the force of the current pulling the debris against the fence during a storm is going to rip the fence loose. As a result, your animals can get out and your neighbor's animals in, a problem whichever way it goes.

Well, a storm gate is nothing more than a section of fence, which is usually made of heavy wire mesh and positioned at the top of the stream banks so that it swings loose on fence posts that are double the normal size. Cables keep the bottom from swinging too far out and staying there, and the bottom is usually made of a fairly heavy log or telephone pole to enable the fence to return to its original position. Such a storm gate will withstand far more battering than a normal fence would. It will also prevent the buildup of debris and the resultant damming of water that eventually floods a lot of fields or rips up several miles of fence line before giving way.

Like fences, gates require more common sense than engineering prowess. When erected with good quality materials and according to basic carpentry rules, they will last many, many years. And besides, the proper planning and construction of one or more gates can be a lot of fun (Illus. 139).

Illus. 139. Horseshoes and wagon wheels combine to make this an attractive gate. A gate must open and close well but doesn't have to be uninteresting.

DECKS

12 · Deck Materials

Although wood and wood products are the primary materials used in the construction of exposed decks, other materials such as fastenings and finishes are also important. Footings used to anchor the posts that support the deck proper are usually concrete. The proper combinations of all materials with good construction details will insure a deck that will provide years of pleasure.

It is the purpose of this book to provide general guides to the proper construction of outdoor wood decks and related units. Illustrations of "poor" as well as "good" practices will be included in many instances.

LUMBER SPECIES AND CHARACTERISTICS

Many lumber species will provide good service in a wood deck. However, some are more adequate for the purpose than others. To select lumber wisely, one must first single out the key requirements of the job. Then it is relatively easy to check the properties of the different woods to see which ones meet these requirements. For example, beams or joists require wood species that are high in bending strength or stiffness; wide boards in railings or fences may best be species that warp little; posts and similar members that are exposed to long wet periods should be heartwood of species with high decay resistance.

The classification of woods commonly used in the United States according to their characteristics is given in Table 1. Follow the recommendations in this table in selecting wood for a specific use in the outdoor structure.

Plywood is a wood product adaptable for use in wood decks and is often recommended for solid deck coverings. Plywood is made in two types—exterior and interior. Only exterior type is recommended where any surface or edge is permanently exposed to the weather. Interior type plywood, even when made with exterior glue and protected on the top surface, is not recommended for such exposures.

Lumber sizes The size of lumber is normally based on green sawn sizes. When the lumber has been dried and surfaced, the finish size (thickness and width) is somewhat less than the sawn size.

The following lumber sizes are those established by the American Lumber Standards Committee.

Nominal (inches)	Dry (inches)	Green (inches)
1	$\frac{3}{4}$	$\frac{25}{32}$
2	$1\frac{1}{2}$	$1\frac{9}{16}$
4	$3\frac{1}{2}$	$3\frac{9}{16}$
6	$5\frac{1}{2}$	$5\frac{5}{8}$
8	$7\frac{1}{4}$	$7\frac{1}{2}$
10	$9\frac{1}{4}$	$9\frac{1}{2}$
12	$11\frac{1}{4}$	$11\frac{1}{2}$

For example, a nominal 2 by 4 would have a surfaced dry size of $1\frac{1}{2}$ by $3\frac{1}{2}$ inches at a maximum moisture content of 19 percent.

Table 1. Broad classification of woods according to characteristics and properties[1]

Kind of wood	Working and behavior characteristics							Strength properties			
	Hardness	Freedom from warping	Ease of working	Paint holding	Nail holding	Decay resistance of heartwood	Proportion of heartwood	Bending strength	Stiffness	Strength as a post	Freedom from pitch
ash	A	B	C	C	A	C	C	A	A	A	A
western red cedar	C	A	A	A	C	A	A	C	C	B	A
cypress	B	B	B	A	B	A	B	B	B	B	A
Douglas fir, larch	B	B	B-C	C	A	B	A	A	A	A	B
gum	B	C	B	C	A	B	B	B	A	B	A
hemlock, white fir[2]	B-C	B	B	C	C	C	C	B	A	B	A
soft pines[3]	C	A	A	A	C	C	B	C	C	C	B
southern pine	B	B	B	C	A	B	C	A	A	A	C
poplar	C	A	B	A	B	C	B	B	B	B	A
redwood	B	A	B	A	B	A	A	B	B	A	A
spruce	C	A-B	B	B	B	C	C	B	B	B	A

[1]A: Among the woods relatively high in the particular respect listed. B: Among woods intermediate in that respect. C: Among woods relatively low in that respect. Letters do not refer to lumber grades.

[2]Includes west coast and eastern hemlocks.

[3]Includes the western and northeastern pines.

Moisture content of wood during fabrication and assembly of a wood frame structure is important. Ideally, it should be about the same moisture content it reaches in service. If green or partially dried wood is used, wood members usually shrink, resulting in poorly fitting joints and loose fastenings after drying has occurred.

Although not as important for exterior use as for interior use, the moisture content of lumber used and exposed to exterior conditions should be considered. The average moisture content of wood exposed to the weather varies with the season, but kiln dried or air dried lumber best fits the midrange of moisture contents that wood reaches in use.

PLYWOOD SPECIFICATIONS

For solid deck applications with direct exposure to the weather, plywood marked C-C Plugged Exterior, or Underlayment Exterior (C-C Plugged) may be specified. Higher grades, such as A-C or B-C Exterior, may also be used. These grades coated with a high-performance wearing surface are commonly used for residential deck areas.

High Density Overlay (HDO) plywood having a hard, phenolic-resin impregnated fibre surface is often used for boat decks with a screened, skid-resistant finish specified. HDO may be painted with standard deck-type paints, if desired, but is usually used without further finish.

Medium Density Overlay (MDO) plywood having a softer resin-fibre overlay requires either a high-performance deck paint, or an elastomeric deck coating system, depending on the intended use.

For premium deck construction, Plyron (plywood with a tempered hardboard face) may be used in conjunction with an elastomeric deck coating.

Plywood specifications for decks are summarized in Table 6 on page 133.

DECAY RESISTANCE OF WOOD

Every material normally used in construction has its distinctive way of deteriorating under adverse conditions. With wood it is decay. Wood will never decay if kept continuously dry (at less than 20-percent moisture content). Because open decks and other outdoor components are exposed to wetting and drying conditions, good drainage, flashings, and similar protective measures are more important in decks than in structures fully protected by a roof.

To provide good performance of wood under exposed conditions, one or more of the following measures should be taken:

(1) Use the heartwood of a decay-resistant species.

(2) Use wood that has been given a good preservative treatment.

(3) Use details that do not trap moisture and that allow easy drainage.

(A combination of (1) and (3), for example, is considered adequate, and (2) is satisfactory alone, but usually at increased cost if pressure treatment is used, or at the expense of increased maintenance if dip or soak treatments are used. Detailing that allows quick drying is always desirable and will be emphasized here).

Frequently, it is cheaper and easier to use a good connecting design than to use an inferior detail with a decay-resistant wood.

Illus. 140. Solid carpeted decks harmonize interior and exterior living areas.

13 · Treatments, Finishes, and Coverings

PRESERVATIVE TREATMENTS

The best treatment of wood to assure long life under severe conditions is pressure preservative treatment. However, most of the wood parts of a deck are exposed only to moderate conditions except at joints and connections. There are two general methods of preservatively treating wood: pressure processes applied commercially according to American Wood-Preservers' Association (AWPA) standards, which provide lasting protection; and nonpressure processes, which normally penetrate the ends and a thin layer of the outer surfaces and require frequent maintenance. The nonpressure processes refer to treatments with water-repellent wood preservatives.

Two general types of preservatives are recommended for severe exterior conditions: oils, such as creosote, or pentachlorophenol in oil or liquified gas carriers; and nonleachable salts, such as the chromated copper arsenates or ammoniacal copper arsenite applied as water solutions.

Poles and posts (severe conditions) Treatment of poles and posts that are in contact with the soil should comply with the latest Federal specification TT-W-571i or with AWPA standards. Insist that the wood material you buy for these purposes has been treated according to these recommended practices.

Lumber and timber for ground and water contact (severe conditions) Wood used under severe conditions, such as ground contact, may be pressure-treated as recommended for poles and posts. However, if cleanliness or paintability is a factor, creosote or pentachlorophenol in heavy oil should not be used. AWPA standards for nonleachable water-borne preservatives and pentachlorophenol in light or volatile petroleum solvents should be selected.

Wood not in contact with ground Where preservative treatment is desirable because the more decay-resistant woods are not available, the use of a more easily applied, less expensive but less effective nonpressure treatment may be considered for joints, connections, and other critical areas. A pentachlorophenol solution with a water repellent is one of the more effective materials of this type. It is available at most lumber or paint dealers as a clear, water-repellent preservative.

These preservatives should be applied by soaking, dipping, or flooding so that end grain, machine cuts, and any existing checks in the wood are well penetrated. Dipping each end of all exterior framing material in water-repellent preservative is recommended, and this should be done after all cutting and drilling is completed. Drilled holes can be easily treated by squirting preservative from an oil can with a long spout. Dry wood absorbs more of these materials than partially dry wood and, consequently, is better protected.

Plywood decks Preservative treatments for plywood decks are covered by the same standards as those for lumber and may be applied by pressure or superficial soaking or dipping. Several types of treatments perform well on plywood; but some deck applications require specific treatments, and the compatibility of the treatment with finish materials should always be checked.

Light, oil-borne preservatives and water-borne preservatives, such as those recommended for lumber, should be used when a clean, odorless, and paintable treatment is required. For maximum service from plywood decks, these preservatives should be pressure-applied.

EXTERIOR FINISHES FOR WOOD

Exterior finishes that might be considered for wood components exposed to the weather include natural finishes, penetrating stains, and paints. In general, natural finishes containing a water repellent and a preservative are preferred over paint for exposed flat surfaces. The natural finishes penetrate the wood and are easily renewed, but paint forms a surface film that may rupture under repeated wetting and drying. Exposed flat surfaces of decks, railings, and stairways are more vulnerable to paint film rupture than are vertical sidewall surfaces. Therefore, a completely satisfactory siding paint may not be suitable for a deck.

Natural finishes (lightly pigmented) are often used for exposed wood decks, railings and stairways, not only because they can be easily renewed but because they enhance the natural color and grain of the wood. Such finishes can be obtained in many colors from a local paint dealer. Light colors are better for deck surfaces subject to traffic, as they show the least contrast in grain color as wear occurs and appearance is maintained longer.

One type of natural finish contains paraffin wax, zinc stearate, penta concentrate, linseed oil, mineral spirits, and tinting colors. Such finishes are manufactured by many leading producers of wood stains and are generally available from paint or lumber dealers.

Penetrating stains (heavily pigmented) for rough and weathered wood may be used on the large sawn members, such as beams and posts. These are similar to the natural finishes just described but contain less oil and more pigment. They are also produced by many companies.

Paint is one of the most widely used finishes for wood. When applied properly over a paintable surface with an initial water-repellent preservative treatment, followed by prime and finish coats, paint is a highly desirable finish for outdoor structures or as an accent color when used with natural finishes. Exposed flat surfaces with end or side joints are difficult to protect with a paint coating unless there is no shrinking or swelling of the wood to rupture the paint film. A crack in the paint film allows water to get beneath the film where is it hard to remove by drying. Retention of such moisture can result in eventual decay.

Good painting practices include an initial application of water-repellent preservative. After allowing two sunny days for drying of the preservative, a prime coat is applied. This can consist of a linseed oil–base paint with pigments that do not contain zinc oxide.

The finish coats can contain zinc oxide pigment and can be of the linseed oil, alkyd, or latex type. Two coats should be used for best results. A three-coat paint job with good-quality paint may last as long as 10 years, when the film is not ruptured by excessive shrinking or swelling of the wood.

COVERINGS AND COATINGS FOR PLYWOOD DECKS

Tough, skid-resistant, elastomeric coatings are available for plywood deck wearing surfaces. These coatings include liquid neoprene, neoprene/Hypalon, and silicone- or rubber-based materials. Plywood joints for these systems are usually sealed with a high performance caulk, such as a silicone or Thiokol (silicone caulks require a primer). Joints may also be covered with a synthetic reinforcing tape, prior to application of the final surface coat, when an elastomeric coating system is used.

Silicone or Thiokol caulks are applied to ¼-inch gaps between plywood panels over some type of filler or "backer" material—such as a foam rod. The caulk "bead" is normally about ¼-inch in diameter. An alternate method is to bevel the panel edges first, and then fill the joint with the caulk before the finish coating is applied.

For a premium quality joint, reinforcing tape is sometimes applied as a flashing over sealed joints. Reinforcing tape can also be used over cant strips at wall-to-deck corner areas and over unsealed plywood joints. For these applications, the tape flashing is embedded in a base coat of the elastomeric deck coating. Specific installation procedures and recommendations are readily available from manufacturers of the various deck coating systems and from the American Plywood Association. Their installation recommendations should be carefully followed.

Where plywood must be installed under wet conditions, the primer or first coat may be applied in the factory or under shelter at the site prior to installation of the panels. In general, the first coat of coating systems for plywood should be applied to a dry, fresh wood surface. Where preservatives are used, the surface should be scraped or sanded to remove any residue produced by the preservative before the prime coat is applied. Finish coats of most systems require a dry clean surface for best results.

If outdoor carpeting is to be used on plywood exposed to the weather, it is advisable to use pressure preservative–treated plywood, with the underside well ventilated, for both low and elevated decks. Since carpeting is relatively new as an exterior surface material, specific information on its long-term performance when used on plywood under severe exposure is not available. Carpet may be readily applied to untreated plywood deck areas that are not subject to repeated wetting.

Canvas is sometimes used as a wearing surface on plywood. It should be installed with a waterproof adhesive, under dry conditions. A canvas surface well fused to the plywood may be painted with regular deck paints.

14 · Deck Design

FRAMING SPANS AND SIZES

The allowable spans for decking, joists and beams and the size of posts depend not only on the size, grade, and spacing of the members but also on the species. Species such as Douglas fir, southern pine, and western larch allow greater spans than some of the less dense pines, cedars, and redwood, for example. Normally, deck members are designed for about the same load as the floors in a dwelling.

The arrangement of the structural members can vary somewhat because of orientation of the deck, position of the house, slope of the lot, etc. However, basically, the beams are supported by the posts (anchored to footings), which in turn support the floor joists (Illus. 141). The deck boards are then fastened to the joists. When beams are spaced more closely together, the joists can be eliminated if the deck boards are thick enough to span between the beams. Railings are located around the perimeter of the deck if required for safety (low-level decks are often constructed without edge railings). When the deck is fastened to the house in some manner, the deck is normally rigid enough to eliminate the need for post bracing. In high free-standing decks, the use of post bracing is good practice.

Post sizes Common sizes for wood posts used in supporting beams and floor framing for wood decks are 4 by 4, 4 by 6, and 6 by 6 inches. The size of the post required is based on the span and spacing of the beams, the load, and the height of the post. Most decks are designed for a live load of 40 pounds per square foot with an additional allowance of 10 pounds per square foot for the weight of the material. The suggested sizes of posts required for various heights under several beam spans and spacings are listed in Table 2. Under normal conditions, the minimum dimension of the post should be the same as the beam width to simplify the method of fastening the two together. Thus a 4- by 8-inch (on edge) beam might use a 4- by 4-inch or a 4- by 6-inch post depending on the height, etc.

Beam spans The nominal sizes of beams for various spacings and spans are listed in Table 3. These sizes are based on such species as Douglas fir, southern pine, and western larch for one group, western hemlock and white fir for a second group, and the soft pines, cedars, spruces, and redwood for a third group. Lumber grade is No. 2 or better.

Joist spans The approximate allowable spans for joists used in outdoor decks are listed in Table 4—both for the denser species of group 1 and the less dense species of groups 2 and 3. These spans are based on strength (40 pounds per square foot live load plus 10 pounds per square foot dead load) with deflection not exceeding 1/360 of span.

Deck board spans Deck boards are mainly used in 2-inch thickness and in widths of 3 and 4 inches. Because deck boards are spaced, spans are normally based on the width of each board as well as its thickness. (Roof decking, with tongue and groove edges and laid up tight, has greater allowable spans than spaced boards.) Decking can also be made of 2- by 3-inch or 2- by 4-inch members placed on edge, or of 1- by 4-inch boards. Deck boards are listed in Table 5.

Plywood decks Spans for plywood decks are shown in Table 6.

Table 2. Minimum post sizes (wood beam supports)[1]

Species group	Post size (in.)	Load area[3] beam spacing × post spacing (sq. ft.)									
		36	48	60	72	84	96	108	120	132	144
1	4 × 4	Up to 12-ft. heights →				Up to 10-ft. heights →			Up to 8-ft. heights →		
	4 × 6					Up to 12-ft. heights →				Up to 10-ft. →	
	6 × 6									Up to 12-ft. →	
2	4 × 4	Up to 12-ft. →		Up to 10-ft. hts. →			Up to 8-ft. heights →				
	4 × 6			Up to 12-ft. hts. →			Up to 10-ft. heights →				
	6 × 6					Up to 12-ft. heights →					
3	4 × 4	Up to 12′	Up to 10′ →		Up to 8-ft. hts. →			Up to 6-ft. heights →			
	4 × 6		Up to 12′ →		Up to 10-ft. hts. →			Up to 8-ft. heights →			
	6 × 6				Up to 12-ft. heights →						

[1]Based on 40 p.s.f. deck live load plus 10 p.s.f. dead load. Grade is Standard and Better for 4- × 4-inch posts and No. 1 and Better for larger sizes.

[2]Group 1: Douglas fir-larch and southern pine. Group 2: Hem-fir and Douglas fir south. Group 3: Western pines and cedars, redwood, and spruces.

[3]Example: If the beam supports are spaced 8 feet, 6 inches, on center and the posts are 11 feet, 6 inches, on center, then the load area is 98. Use next larger area 108.

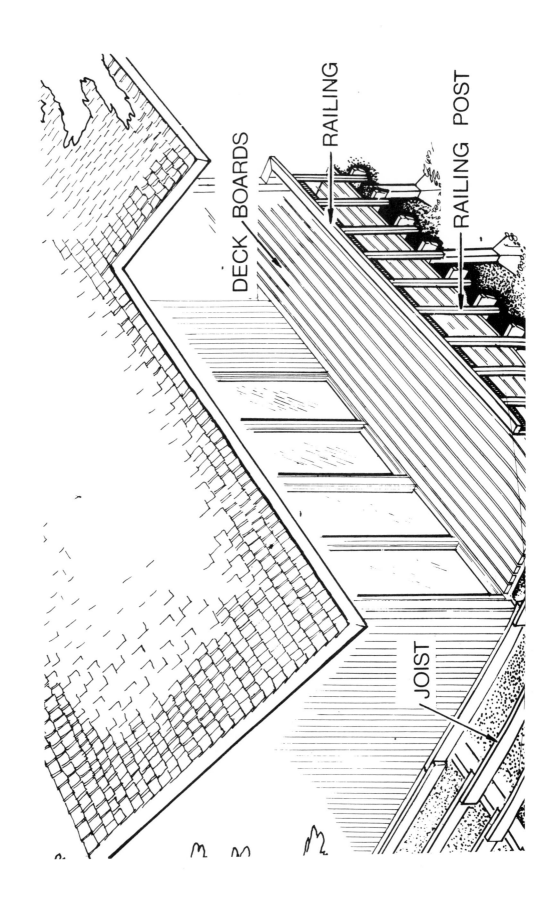

DECK BOARDS

RAILING

RAILING POST

JOIST

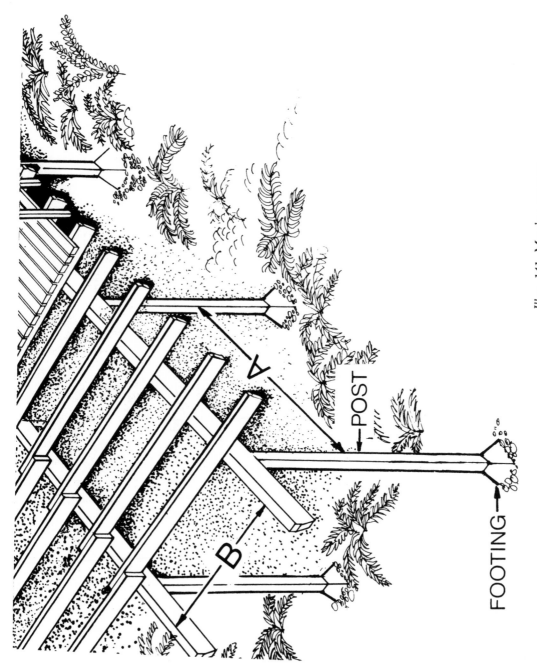

POST

FOOTING

Illus. 141. Member arrangement in a wood deck.

Table 3. Minimum beam sizes and spans[1]

Note: In the original, each "Up to …" value is drawn as a horizontal arrow spanning a range of beam-spacing columns. The readings below place each value at its column position; arrows (→) indicate the span extends across adjacent spacing columns.

Species group[2] 1

Beam size (in.)	Spacing between beams[3] (ft.) 4	5	6	7	8	9	10	11	12
4 × 6	Up to 6-ft. spans →								
3 × 8	Up to 8-ft. →			Up to 6-ft. spans →					
4 × 8		Up to 10'	Up to 8' →			Up to 6-ft. spans →			
3 × 10		Up to 11'	Up to 9'	Up to 7-ft. →				Up to 6-ft.	
4 × 10		Up to 12'	Up to 10'	Up to 8-ft. →				Up to 7-ft.	
3 × 12		Up to 12'	Up to 11'	Up to 10'	Up to 9-ft. →		Up to 8-ft. spans →		
4 × 12			Up to 12'		Up to 11'	Up to 10'		Up to 9-ft. →	
6 × 10				Up to 12'		Up to 11'	Up to 10-ft. spans →		
6 × 12						Up to 12-ft. spans →			

Species group[2] 2

Beam size (in.)	Spacing between beams[3] (ft.) 4	5	6	7	8	9	10	11	12
4 × 6	Up to 6-ft. →								
3 × 8	Up to 7-ft. →		Up to 6-ft. →						
4 × 8		Up to 9'	Up to 7-ft. →		Up to 6-ft. →				
3 × 10		Up to 10'	Up to 8'	Up to 7-ft. →		Up to 6-ft. spans →			
4 × 10		Up to 11'	Up to 9'	Up to 8-ft. →		Up to 7-ft. spans →			Up to 6'
3 × 12		Up to 12'	Up to 10'	Up to 9'		Up to 8-ft. →	Up to 7-ft. spans →		
4 × 12		Up to 12'	Up to 11'	Up to 10'		Up to 9-ft. →		Up to 8-ft. →	
6 × 10				Up to 11'	Up to 10-ft. →		Up to 9-ft. spans →		
6 × 12				Up to 12'		Up to 11-ft. →		Up to 10' →	

Group	Beam size					
3	4×6	Up to 6'				
	3×8	Up to 7'	Up to 6'			
	4×8	Up to 8'	Up to 7'	Up to 6-ft.		
	3×10	Up to 9'	Up to 8'	Up to 7'	Up to 6-ft. spans	
	4×10	Up to 10'	Up to 9'	Up to 8-ft.	Up to 7-ft.	Up to 6-ft. spans
	3×12	Up to 11'	Up to 10'	Up to 9'	Up to 7-ft. spans	Up to 6-ft.
	4×12	Up to 12'	Up to 11'	Up to 10'	Up to 8-ft.	Up to 7-ft.
	6×10		Up to 12'	Up to 11'	Up to 9-ft.	Up to 8-ft. spans
	6×12		Up to 12-ft.	Up to 11'	Up to 10-ft.	Up to 8'

[1] Beams are on edge. Spans are center to center distances between posts or supports. (Based on 40 p.s.f. deck live load plus 10 p.s.f. dead load. Grade is No. 2 or Better; No. 2, medium grain southern pine.)

[2] Group 1: Douglas fir-larch and southern pine. Group 2: Hem-fir and Douglas fir south. Group 3: Western pines and cedars, redwood, and spruces.

[3] Example: If the beams are 9 feet, 8 inches apart and the species is Group 2, use the 10-ft. column; 3×10 up to 6-ft. spans, 4×10 or 3×12 up to 7-ft. spans, 4×12 or 6×10 up to 9-ft. spans, 6×12 up to 11-ft. spans.

Table 4. Maximum allowable spans for deck joists[1]

Species group[2]	Joist size (inches)	Joist spacing (inches)		
		16	24	32
1	2 × 6	9'-9"	7'-11"	6'-2"
	2 × 8	12'-10"	10'-6"	8'-1"
	2 × 10	16'-5"	13'-4"	10'-4"
2	2 × 6	8'-7"	7'-0"	5'-8"
	2 × 8	11'-4"	9'-3"	7'-6"
	2 × 10	14'-6"	11'-10"	9'-6"
3	2 × 6	7'-9"	6'-2"	5'-0"
	2 × 8	10'-2"	8'-1"	6'-8"
	2 × 10	13'-0"	10'-4"	8'-6"

[1]Joists are on edge. Spans are center to center distances between beams or supports. Based on 40 p.s.f. deck live loads plus 10 p.s.f. dead load. Grade is No. 2 or Better; No. 2 medium grain southern pine.

[2]Group 1: Douglas fir-larch and southern pine. Group 2: Hem-fir and Douglas fir south. Group 3: Western pines and cedars, redwood, and spruces.

Table 5. Maximum allowable spans for spaced deck boards[1]

Species group[2]	Maximum allowable span (inches)[3]					
	Laid flat				Laid on edge	
	1 × 4	2 × 2	2 × 3	2 × 4	2 × 3	2 × 4
1	16	60	60	60	90	144
2	14	48	48	48	78	230
3	12	42	42	42	66	108

[1]These spans are based on the assumption that more than one floor board carries normal loads. If concentrated loads are a rule, spans should be reduced accordingly.

[2]Group 1: Douglas fir-larch and southern pine. Group 2: Hem-fir and Douglas fir south. Group 3: Western pines and cedars, redwood, and spruces.

[3]Based on Construction grade or Better (Select Structural, Appearance, No. 1 or No. 2).

FASTENERS

The strength and utility of any wood structure or component are in great measure dependent upon the fastenings used to hold the parts together. The most common wood fasteners are nails and spikes, followed by screws, lag screws, bolts, and metal connectors and straps of various shapes. An important factor for outdoor use of fasteners is the finish selected. Metal fasteners should be rust-proofed in some manner or made of rust-resistant metals. Galvanized and cadmium plated finishes are the most common. Aluminum, stainless steel, copper, brass, and other rust-proof fasteners are

Table 6. Recommended grades, minimum thicknesses, and nailing details for various spans and species groups of plywood decking[1]

Plywood species group[2]	Panel thicknesses in inches[3] For maximum spacings between supports (inches)			
	16	20	24	32 or 48
1	½	⅝	¾	1⅛
2 & 3	⅝	¾	⅞	1⅛
4	¾	⅞	1	5

[1]*Recommended thicknesses are based on Underlayment Exterior (C-C Plugged) grade. Higher grades, such as A-C or B-C Exterior, may be used. 19/32-inch plywood may be substituted for 5/8-inch and 23/32-inch for 3/4-inch.*

[2]*Plywood species groups are approximately the same but not identical to those shown for lumber in Tables 2-5. Therefore, in selecting plywood, one should be guided by the group number stamped on the panel.*

[3]*Edges of panels shall be T&G or supported by blocking.*

[4]*Nailing details: Size: 6[d] deformed shank nails, except 8[d] for 7/8-inch or 1-1/8-inch plywood on spans 24 to 48 inches. Spacing: 6 inches along panel edges, 10 inches along intermediate supports (6 inches for 48-inch on center supports). Corrosion resistant nails are recommended where nail heads are to be exposed. Nails should be set 1/16 inch (1/8 inch for 1 1/8-inch plywood).*

[5]*Not permitted.*

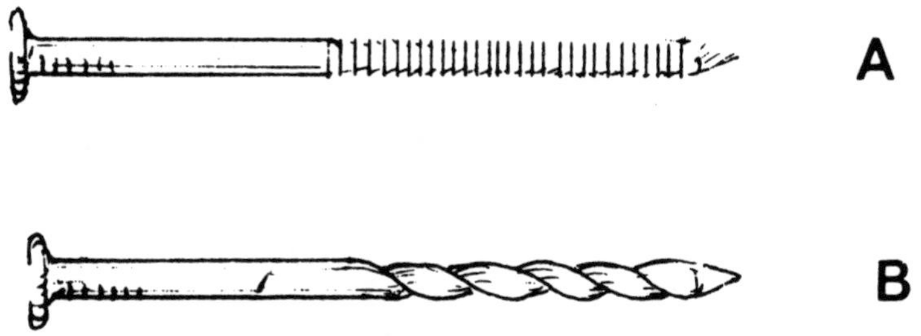

A

B

Illus. 142. Deformed shank nails. A: Annular grooved (ring shank). B: Spirally grooved.

also satisfactory. The most successful for such species as redwood are hot-dip galvanized, aluminum, or stainless steel fasteners. These prevent staining of the wood under exposed conditions. A rusted nail, washer, or bolt head is not only unsightly but difficult to remove and replace. They are often a factor in the loss of strength of the connection.

Among the nails, smooth shank nails often lose their holding power when exposed to wetting and drying cycles. The best assurance of a high retained withdrawal resistance is the use of a deformed shank nail or spike. The two general types most satisfactory are the annular grooved (ring shank) and the spirally grooved nail (Illus. 142). The value of such a nail or spike is its capacity to retain withdrawal resistance even after repeated wetting and drying cycles. Such nails should be used for the construction of exposed units if screws, lag screws, or bolts are not used.

Nail length is often designated by penny (d) size. The letter "d" is the English symbol for pound. It also means penny in the English monetary system. The theory is that penny size represented the number of pounds a thousand nails weighed. Today this antiquated system represents only the length of nails. It does **NOT** indicate count per pound, diameter, style and size head, or other characteristics.

Table 7. Penny size conversion chart

PENNY SIZE	2d	3d	4d	5d	6d	7d	8d	9d	10d	12d
LENGTH— INCHES	1″	1¼″	1½″	1¾″	2″	2¼″	2½″	2¾″	3″	3¼″

PENNY SIZE	16d	20d	30d	40d	50d	60d	70d	80d	90d	100d
LENGTH— INCHES	3½″	4″	4½″	5″	5½″	6″	7″	8″	9″	10″

Wood screws may be used if cost is not a factor in areas where nails are normally specified. Wood screws retain their withdrawal resistance to a great extent under adverse conditions. They are also superior to nails when end-grain fastening must be used. Because of their larger diameter, screw length need not be as great as a deformed shank nail. The flathead screw is best for exposed surfaces because it does not extend beyond the surface (Illus. 143), and the oval head protrudes less than the round head screw. This is an important factor in the construction of tables and benches. The use of a lead hole about three-fourths the diameter of the screw is good practice, especially in the denser woods to prevent splitting. Screws should always be turned in their full length and not driven part way. The new variable speed drills (with a screwdriver) are excellent for applying screws. **Lag screws** are commonly used to fasten a relatively thick, such as 2- by 6-inch, member to a thicker member (3-or-more-inch) where a through bolt cannot be used. Lead holes must be used, and the lag screw turned in its entire length. Use a large washer under the head. Lead holes for the threaded portion should be about two-thirds the diameter of the lag screw for the softer woods such as redwood or cedar, and three-fourths the diameter for the dense hardwoods and for such species as Douglas fir. The lead hole for the unthreaded shank of the lag screw should be the same diameter as that of the lag screw.

Bolts are one of the most rigid fasteners in a simple form. They may be used for small connections such as railings-to-posts and for large members when combined with timber connectors. The two types of bolts most commonly used in light frame construction are the carriage bolt and the machine bolt (Illus. 144). When obtainable, the step bolt is preferred over the carriage bolt because of its larger head diameter.

The carriage bolt is normally used without a washer under the head. A squared section at the bolt head resists turning as it is tightened. Washers should always be used under the head of the machine bolt and under the nut of both types. Bolt holes should be the exact diameter of the bolt. When a bolt-fastened member is loaded, such as a beam to a post, the bearing strength of the wood under the bolt is important as well as the strength of the bolt. A larger diameter bolt or several smaller diameter bolts may be used when the softer woods are involved. Crushing of wood under the head of a carriage bolt or under the washer of any bolt should always be avoided. The use of larger washers and a washer under the carriage bolt head is advisable when the less dense wood species are used.

Miscellaneous fastening methods in addition to the nail, screw, and bolt are also used for fastening wood members together, or to other materials. Although split ring connectors and similar fasteners are normally used for large beams or trusses, other connectors may be used to advantage in the construction of a wood deck. These include metal anchors for connecting posts to concrete footings; angle iron and special connectors for fastening posts to beams; joist hangers and metal strapping for fastening joists to beams; and others. While research has not advanced far enough as yet, the new mastic adhesives are showing promise for field assembly of certain wood members. Such materials used alone or with metal fasteners will likely result in longer-lived connections.

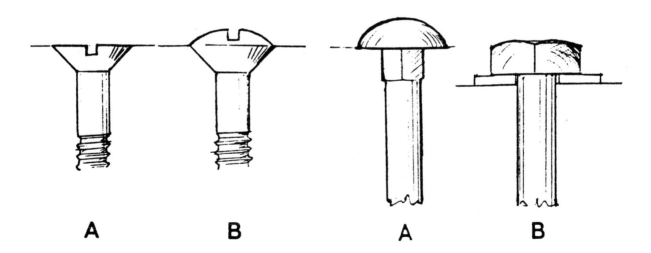

A   **B**   **A**   **B**

Illus. 143 (left). Wood screws. A: Flat head. B: Oval head. Illus. 144 (right). Bolts. A: Carriage. B: Machine.

15 · General Rules for Deck Construction

Our experience with exposed deck construction can be summarized in the following general guides for the use of wood and fasteners in outdoor decks.

GUIDES FOR FASTENER USE

- Use non-staining fasteners.
- Always fasten a thinner member to a thicker member (unless clinched nails are used).
  - A nail should be long enough to penetrate the receiving member a distance twice the thickness of the thinner member but not less than 1½ inches (for example, for a ¾-inch board, the nail should penetrate the receiving member 1½ inches. Use at least a 7-penny nail).
  - A screw should be long enough to penetrate the receiving member at least the thickness of the thinner (outside) member but with not less than a 1-inch penetration (for example, fastening a ¾-inch member to a 2 by 4 would require a 1¾-inch-long screw).
- To reduce splitting of boards when nailing:
  - Blunt the nail point.
  - Predrill (three-fourths of nail diameter).
  - Use smaller diameter nails and a greater number.
  - Use greater spacing between nails.
  - Stagger nails in each row.
  - Place nails no closer to edge than one-half of the board thickness and no closer to end than the board thickness.
  - In wide boards (8 inches or more), do not place nails close to edge.

- Use minimum of two nails per board—for example, two nails for 4- and 6-inch widths and three nails for 8- and 10-inch widths.
- Avoid end grain nailing. When unavoidable, use screws or side grain wood cleat adjacent to end-grain member (as a post).
- Lag screw use:
  - Use a plain, flat washer under the head.
  - Use lead hole and turn in full distance; do not overturn.
  - Do not countersink (reduces wood section).
- Bolt use:
  - Use flat washers under nut and head of machine bolts and under nut of

Illus. 145. Decks expand living areas on steep hillsides with little disturbance of the ground.

carriage bolt. In softer woods, use larger washer under carriage bolt heads.

- Holes to be exact size of bolt diameter.

GUIDES FOR OUTDOOR WOOD USE

- When a wide member is required, use edge-grain boards, as they shrink, swell, and cup less than flat-grain boards during moisture changes.
- Do not use wood in direct contact with soil unless members are pressure-treated.
- Provide clearance of wood members (such as fences and posts) from plant growth and ground to minimize high moisture content. Bottoms of posts, when supported by piers for example, should be 6 inches above the grade.
- Use forms of flat members that provide natural drainage (a sloped top of a cap rail, for example).
- Use rectangular sections with width and thickness as nearly equal as possible, such as 3 by 4 instead of 2 by 6.
- Dip all ends and points of fabrication in a water-repellent preservative treatment prior to placement.

16 · Deck Construction

SITE PREPARATION

Grading and drainage Site preparation for construction of a wood deck is often less costly than that for a concrete terrace. When the site is steep, it is difficult to grade and to treat the back slopes in preparing a base for the concrete slab. In grading the site for a wood deck, one must normally consider only proper drainage, disturbing the natural terrain as little as possible. Grading should be enough to insure water runoff, usually just a minor leveling of the ground.

Often, absorption of the soil under an open deck with spaced boards will account for a good part of a moderate rainfall. If the deck also serves as a roof for a garage, carport, or living area below, drainage should be treated as a part of the house roof drainage, whether by gutters, downspouts, or drip and drain pockets at the ground level. In such cases, some form of drainage may be required to carry water away from the site and prevent erosion. This can usually be accomplished with drain tile laid in a shallow drainage ditch. Tile should be spaced and joints covered with a strip of asphalt felt before the trench is filled. The tile can lead to a dry well or to a drainage field beyond the site. Perforated cement or plastic tile is also available for this use.

Weed and growth control There may also be a need for control of weed growth beneath the deck. Without some control or deterrent, such growth can lead to high moisture content of wood members and subsequent decay hazards where decks are near the grade. Common methods for such control consist of (a) the application of a weed killer to the plants or (b) the use of a membrane such as 4- or 6-mil polyethylene or 30-pound asphalt saturated felt. Such coverings should be placed just before the deck boards are laid. Stones, bricks or other permanent means of anchoring the membranes in place should be used around the perimeter and in any interior surface variations that may be present. A few holes should be punched in the covering so that a good share of the rain will not run off and cause erosion.

FOOTINGS

Some type of footing is required to support the posts or poles that transfer the deck loads to the ground. In simplest form, the bottom of a treated pole and the friction of the earth around the pole provide this support. More commonly, however, some type of masonry, usually concrete, is used as a footing upon which the poles or posts rest. Several footing systems are normally used, some more preferred than others.

Footings for posts below grade Footings required for support of vertical members such as wood poles or posts must be designed to carry the load of the deck superstructure. In a simple form, the design includes the use of pressure-treated posts or poles embedded to a depth that provides sufficient bearing and rigidity (Illus. 147). This may require a depth of 3 to 5 feet or more, depending on the exposed pole height and applied loads. This type is perhaps more commonly used for pole structures such as storage sheds or barns. In areas where frost is a problem, such as in the northern part of the United States, an embedment depth of 4 feet is commonly a minimum. But a lesser depth may be adequate in warmer climates. Soil should be well-tamped around the pole.

Concrete footings below the surface are normally used for treated posts or poles. Two such types may be used. The first consists of a prepoured footing upon which the wood members rest (Illus. 148). Embedment depth should be only enough to provide lateral resistance, usually 2 to 3 feet. The exception is in cold climates where frost may penetrate to a depth of 4 feet or more. Minimum size for concrete footings in normal soils should be 12 by 12 by 8 inches. Where spacing of the poles is over about 6 feet, 20 by 20 by 10 inches or larger sizes are preferred. However, soil capacities should be determined before design.

Another type of below-grade footing is the poured-in-place type shown in Illus. 149. In such construction, the poles are prealigned, plumbed, and supported above the bottom of the excavated hole. Concrete is then poured below and around the butt end of the pole. A minimum thickness of 8 inches of concrete below the bottom of the pole is advisable. Soil may be added above the concrete when necessary for protection in cold weather. Such footings do not require tamped soil around the pole to provide lateral resistance. All poles or posts embedded in the soil should always be pressure-treated for long life.

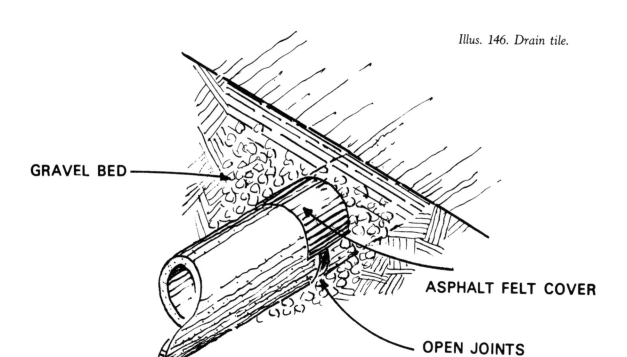

Illus. 146. Drain tile.

GRAVEL BED

ASPHALT FELT COVER

OPEN JOINTS

CEMENT OR TILE DRAIN PIPE

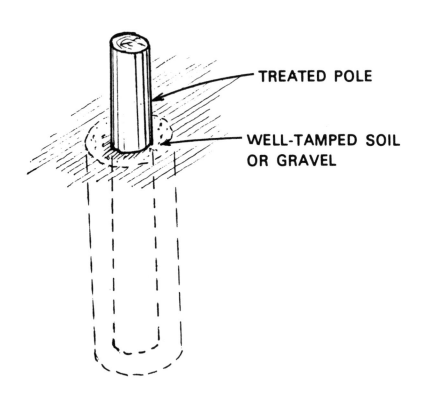

Illus. 147. Pole without footing.

TREATED POLE

WELL-TAMPED SOIL OR GRAVEL

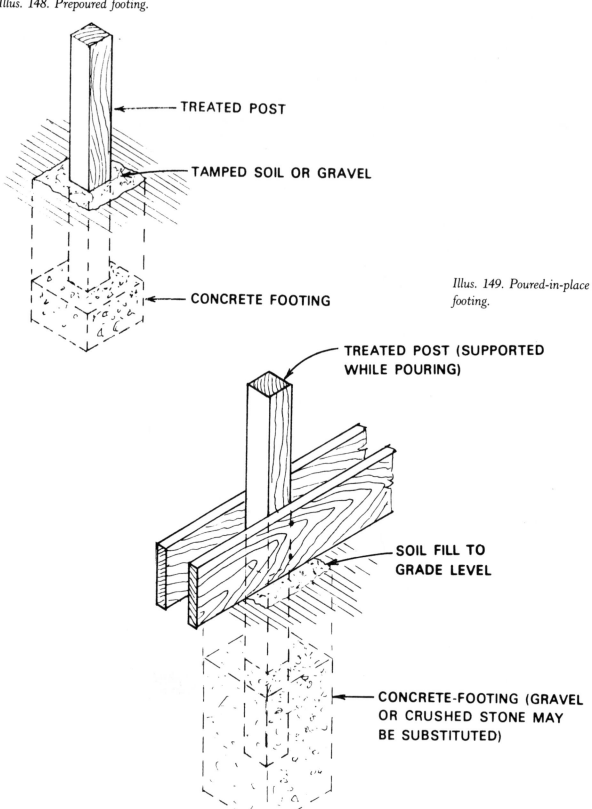

Illus. 148. Prepoured footing.

TREATED POST

TAMPED SOIL OR GRAVEL

Illus. 149. Poured-in-place footing.

CONCRETE FOOTING

TREATED POST (SUPPORTED WHILE POURING)

SOIL FILL TO GRADE LEVEL

CONCRETE-FOOTING (GRAVEL OR CRUSHED STONE MAY BE SUBSTITUTED)

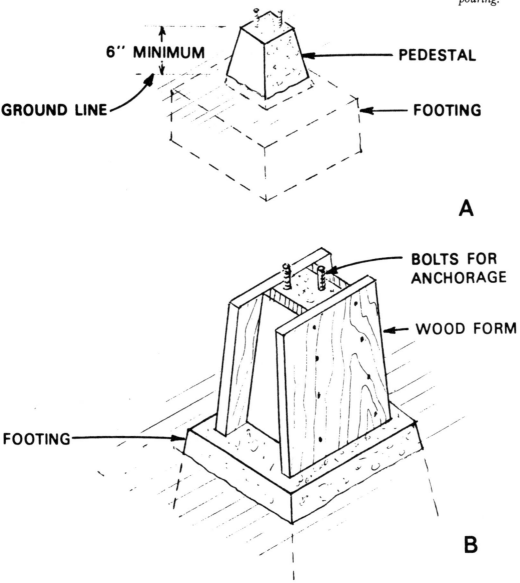

6″ MINIMUM

GROUND LINE

PEDESTAL

FOOTING

A

BOLTS FOR ANCHORAGE

WOOD FORM

FOOTING

B

Footings for posts above grade Footings or footing extensions for posts that are entirely exposed above the grade are poured so the top is at least 6 inches above the surrounding soil. When the size of the footing is greater than the post size (which is normal), a pedestal-type extension is often used (Illus. 150A). The bottom of the footing should be located below frost level, which may require a long pier-type pedestal. A wood form can be used when pouring pedestal (Illus. 150B). Made in this manner with extension on each side, it is easily demountable. The use of form nails (double-head) is also satisfactory. Bolts, angle irons, or other post anchorage should be placed when pouring, and anchor bolts or other bond bars should extend into the footing for positive anchorage against uplift.

POST-TO-FOOTING ANCHORAGE

The anchorage of supporting posts to footings with top surfaces above grade is important as they should not only resist lateral movement but also uplift stresses that can occur during periods of high winds. These anchorages should be designed for good drainage and freedom from contact of the end grain of the wood with wet concrete. This is advisable to prevent decay or damage to the bottom of the wood post. It is also important that the post ends be given a dip treatment of water-repellent preservative. Unfortunately, such features are sometimes lacking in post anchorage. As recommended for nails, screws, bolts, and other fastenings, all metal anchors should be galvanized or treated in some manner to resist corrosion. **Poor design** includes an embedded wood block as a fastening member with the post toenailed in place (Illus. 151A). This is generally poor practice even when the block has been pressure treated, as moisture can accumulate in the post bottom.

Another poor practice is shown in Illus. 151B. The bottom of the post is in direct contact with the concrete footing, which can result in moisture absorption. Although the pin anchor resists lateral movement, it has little uplift resistance.

Illus. 151. Post-to-footing anchorage. A and B—Poor practice.

Better design of Illus. 152A is a slight improvement over Illus. 151B as a heavy roofing paper and roofing mastic prevents the bottom of the post from absorbing moisture from the concrete footing.

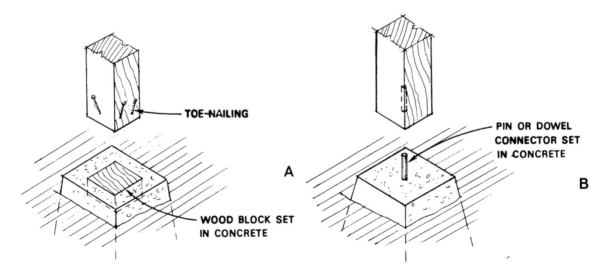

TOE-NAILING

WOOD BLOCK SET IN CONCRETE

A

PIN OR DOWEL CONNECTOR SET IN CONCRETE

B

A better system of anchoring small 4- by 4-inch posts is shown in Illus. 152B. In such anchorage, a galvanized lag screw is turned into the bottom of the post with a large square washer (about 3- by 3- by ¼-inch thick for a 4- by 4-inch post) placed for a bearing area. Post is then anchored into a grouted predrilled hole or supported in place while concrete is poured. The washer prevents direct contact with the concrete and prevents moisture wicking into the bottom of the post, and the lag screw head provides some uplift resistance.

Illus. 152. Post-to-footing anchorage. A and B— Improved practice.

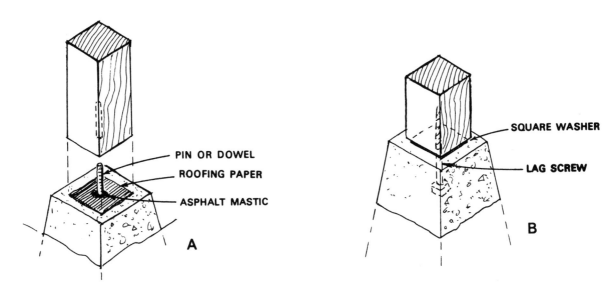

PIN OR DOWEL
ROOFING PAPER
ASPHALT MASTIC
A

SQUARE WASHER
LAG SCREW
B

Good design is an anchorage system for supporting small posts, beams, stair treads, and similar members, utilizing a small steel pipe (galvanized or painted) with a pipe flange at each end (Illus. 153A). A welded plate or angle iron can be substituted for the pipe flange (Illus. 153B). The pipe flange or plate-to-post connection should be made with large screws or lag screws. The flange can be fastened to the post bottom and turned in place after the concrete is poured (Illus. 153A). When an angle iron is used, the entire assembly is poured in place. A good anchor for beams used in low decks is shown in Illus. 153C.

Other post anchors can be obtained (or made up) for anchoring wood posts to a masonry base. Such anchors are normally used for solid 4- by 4-inch or larger posts. All are designed to provide lateral as well as uplift resistance. Some means, such as a plate or supporting angle, is provided to prevent contact of the post with the concrete, thus reducing the chances for decay. All holes drilled into posts for the purpose of anchorage should be flushed with a water-repellent preservative to provide protection. An oil can is a good method of applying such materials.

One type of anchor is shown in Illus. 154. Post support is supplied by the

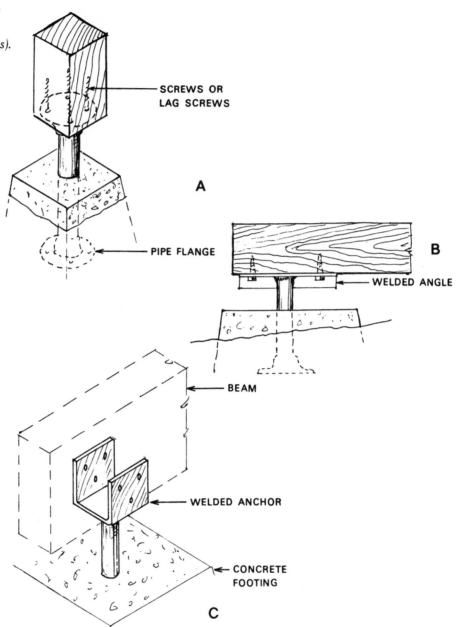

Illus. 153. Pipe and flange anchor. A: Pipe flange. B: Welded angle (low decks). C: Saddle anchor for low decks.

SCREWS OR LAG SCREWS

A

PIPE FLANGE

B

WELDED ANGLE

BEAM

WELDED ANCHOR

CONCRETE FOOTING

C

anchor itself. This step-flange anchor is positioned while the concrete is being poured and should be located so that the bottom of the post is about 2 inches above the concrete.

Another type of anchor for solid posts consists of a heavy metal strap shaped in the form of a "U" with or without a bearing plate welded between (Illus. 155). These anchors are placed as the concrete pier or slab is being poured. As shown in Illus. 154, the post is held in place with bolts.

Illus. 156 illustrates one type of anchor that may be used with double posts. In this and similar cases, the anchor in the concrete is positioned during the pouring operation.

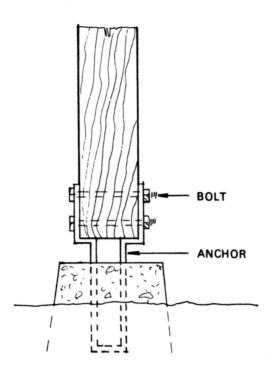

Illus. 154. Step-flange anchor.

BOLT

ANCHOR

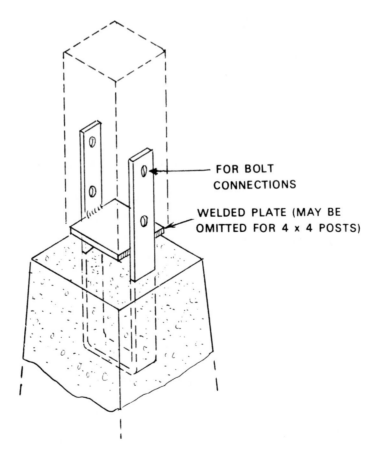

Illus. 155. Double post anchor (without bearing plate).

FOR BOLT CONNECTIONS

WELDED PLATE (MAY BE OMITTED FOR 4 x 4 POSTS)

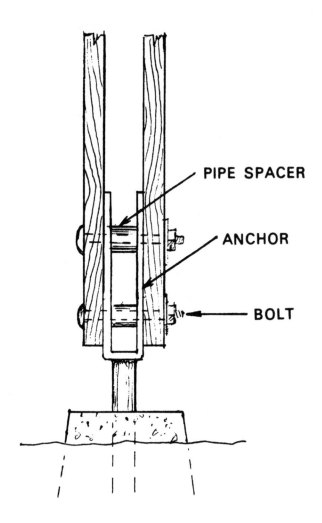

PIPE SPACER

ANCHOR

BOLT

BEAM-TO-POST CONNECTION

Beams are members to which the floor boards are directly fastened or which support a system of joists. Such beams must be fastened to the supporting posts. Beams may be single large or small members or consist of two smaller members fastened to each side of the posts. When a solid deck is to be constructed, the beams should be sloped at least 1 inch in 8 to 10 feet away from the house.

Single beams when 4 inches or wider usually bear on a post. When this system is used, the posts must be trimmed evenly so that the beam bears on all posts. Use a line level or other method to establish this alignment.

A simple but poor method of fastening a 4- by 4-inch post to a 4- by 8-inch beam, for example, is by toe-nailing (Illus. 157A). This is poor practice and should be avoided. Splitting can occur, which reduces the strength of the joint. It is also inadequate in resisting twisting of the beam.

A better system is by the use of a 1- by 4-inch lumber or plywood (exterior grade) cleat located on two sides of the post (Illus. 157B). Cleats are nailed to the beam and post with 7^{d} or 8^{d} deformed shank nails.

A good method of post-to-beam connection is by the use of a metal angle at each side (Illus. 158A). A 3- by 3-inch angle or larger should be used so that fasteners can be turned in easily. Use lag screws to fasten them in place. A metal strap fastened to the beam and the post might also be

Illus. 157. Beam-to-post connection. A: Toe-nailing, a poor practice. B: Better practice is to use cleat.

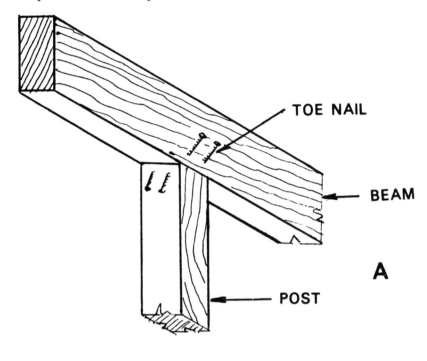

TOE NAIL

BEAM

POST

A

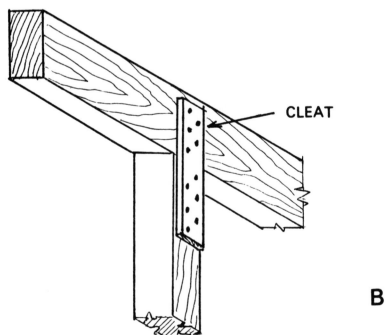

CLEAT

B

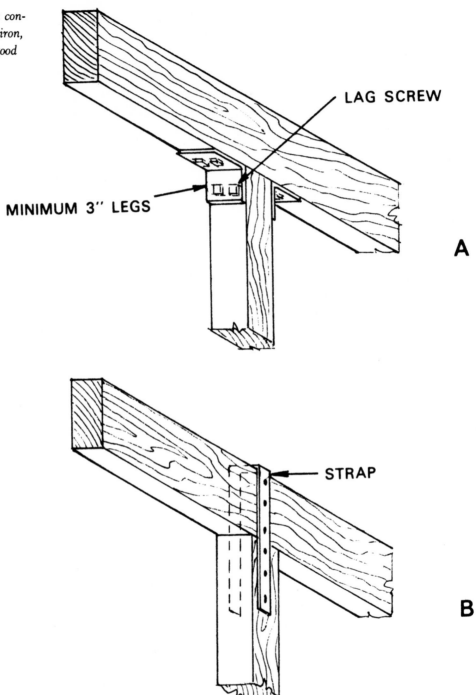

Illus. 158. Beam-to-post connection. Both A, angle iron, and B, strapping, are good methods.

LAG SCREW

MINIMUM 3" LEGS

A

STRAP

B

used for single beams (Illus. 158B). A ⅛- by 3-inch or larger strap, pre-formed to insure a good fit, will provide an adequate connection. Use 10^d deformed shank nails for the smaller members and ¼-inch lag screws for larger members.

A good method of connection for smaller posts and beams consists of a sheet metal flange that is formed to provide fastening surfaces to both beam and post (Illus. 159A). The flange is normally fastened with 8^d nails. To prevent splitting, nails should not be located too close to the end of the post. Upper edges of this connector can collect and retain moisture, but this weakness can be minimized somewhat by providing a small groove along the beam for the flange (Illus. 159B).

When a **double post** is used, such as two 2- by 6-inch members, a single

Illus. 159. Metal flange. A: Flange in place. B: Groove in beam.

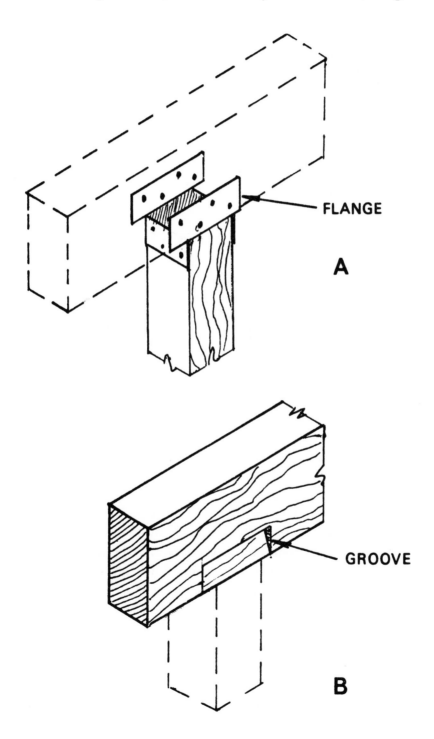

FLANGE

A

GROOVE

B

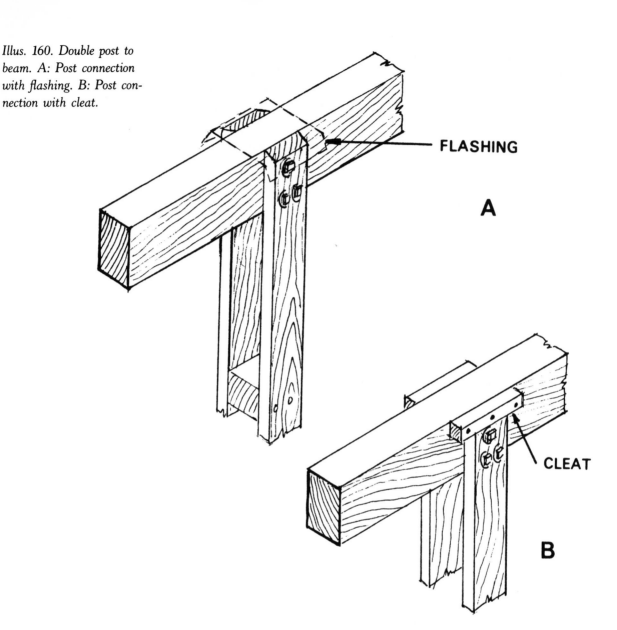

Illus. 160. Double post to beam. A: Post connection with flashing. B: Post connection with cleat.

FLASHING

A

CLEAT

B

beam is usually placed between them. One method of terminating the post ends is shown in Illus. 160A. This is not fully satisfactory as the end grain of the posts is exposed. Some protection can be had by placing asphalt felt or metal flashing over the joint. Fastening is done with bolts or lag screws. Another method of protection is by the use of cleats over the ends of the posts (Illus. 160B).

Double or split beams are normally bolted to the top of the posts, one on each side (Illus. 161A). As brought out previously, the load capacity of such a bolted joint depends on the bolt diameter, the number of bolts used, and the resistance of the wood under the bolts. Thus larger diameter bolts should be used to provide greater resistance for the less dense woods (for example, ½-inch rather than ⅜-inch diameter). Notching the top of the beam as shown in Illus. 161B provides greater load capacity. A piece of asphalt felt or a metal flashing over the joint will provide some protection for the post end.

Small single beams are occasionally used with larger dimension posts (for example, 4- by 8-inch beam and 6- by 6-inch post). In such cases, one method of connection consists of bolting the beam directly to the supporting posts (Illus. 162A). Some type of flashing should be used over the end of the post.

Illus. 161. Double beam to post. A: Bolted joint with flashing. B: Notched and bolted joint with flashing.

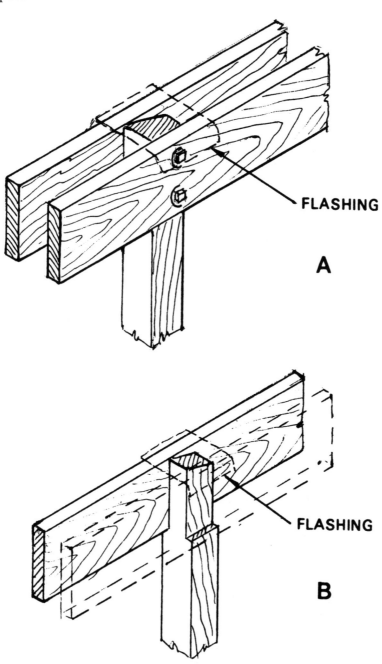

FLASHING

A

FLASHING

B

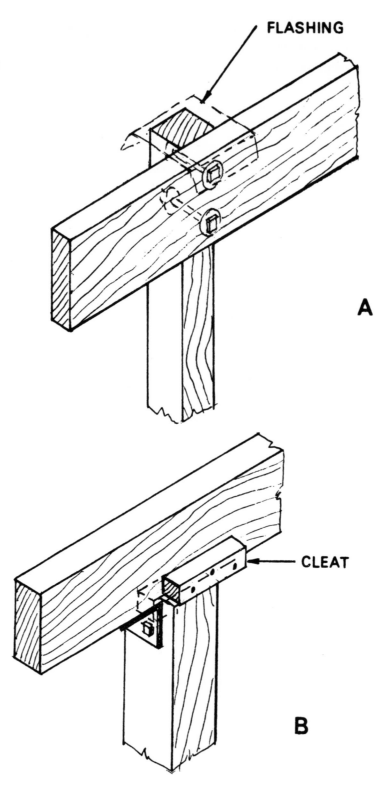

Illus. 162. Small beam to post. A: Bolted connection. B: Good connection for large post. C (next page): Extension of post for rail.

FLASHING

A

CLEAT

B

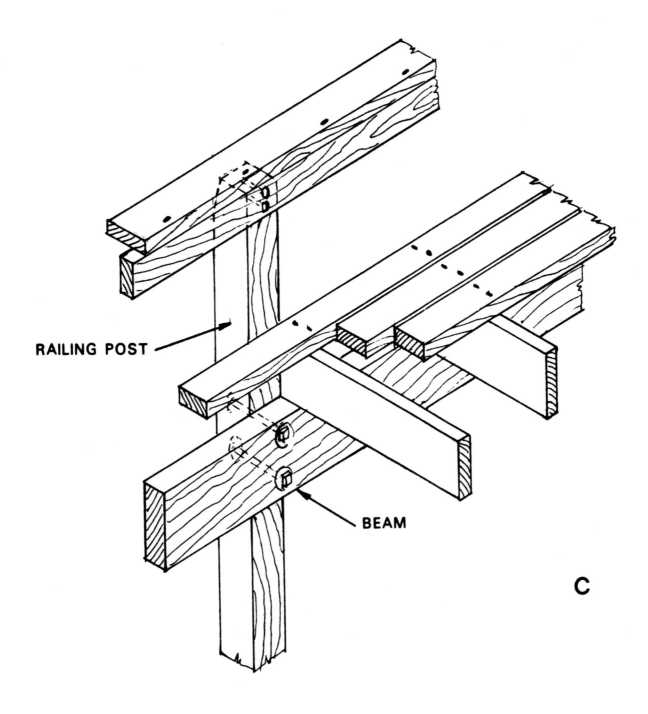

RAILING POST

BEAM

C

Another method of connecting smaller beams to larger posts is shown in Illus. 162B. A short section of angle iron is used on each side of the post for anchorage and a wood cleat is then placed to protect the exposed end grain of the larger post.

It is sometimes advantageous to use the post that supports the beam as a railing post. In such a design, the beam is bolted to the post that extends above the deck to support the railing members (Illus. 162C).

BEAM-AND-JOIST-TO-HOUSE CONNECTIONS

When the deck is adjacent to the house, some method of connecting beams or joists to the house is normally required. This may consist of supporting such members through metal hangers, wood ledgers or angle irons, or utilizing the top of the masonry foundation or basement wall. It is usually good practice to design the deck so that the top of the deck boards are just under the sill of the door leading to the deck. This will provide protection from rains as well as easy access to the deck.

Beams One method of connecting the beam to the house consists of the use of metal beam hangers (Illus. 163A). These may be fastened directly to a floor framing member, such as a joist header, or to a 2- by 8-inch or 2- by 10-inch member that has been bolted or lagscrewed to the house framing. Use 6-penny or longer nails or the short, large-diameter nails often furnished with commercial hangers for fastening. Hangers are available for all beams up to 6 by 14 inches in size. In new construction, beam pockets or spaces between floor framing headers can be provided for the deck beam support. Beams can also be secured to the house proper by bearing on ledgers that have been anchored to the floor framing or to the masonry wall with expansion shields and lag screws. The beam should be fastened to the ledger or to the house with a framing anchor or a small metal angle (Illus. 163B).

Joists When joists of the deck are perpendicular to the side or end of the house, they are connected in much the same manner as beams except that fasteners are smaller. The use of a ledger lag-screwed to the house is shown in Illus. 164A. Joists are toe-nailed to the ledger and the house (header or stringer joists) or fastened with small metal clips.

Joists can also be fastened by a 2- by 8-inch or 2- by 10-inch member (lag-screwed to the house) by means of joist hangers (Illus. 164B). Six-penny nails or 1¼-inch galvanized roofing nails are used to fasten the hangers to the joist and to the header. When joists or beams are parallel to the house, no ledger or other fastening member is normally required (Illus. 164C). If they are supported by beams, the beams, of course, are then connected to the house, as previously illustrated.

BRACING

On uneven sites or sloping lots, posts are often 5 or more feet in height. When the deck is free (not attached to the house), it is good practice to use bracing between posts to provide lateral resistance. Treated poles or posts embedded in the soil or in concrete footings usually have sufficient resistance to lateral forces, and such construction normally requires no addi-

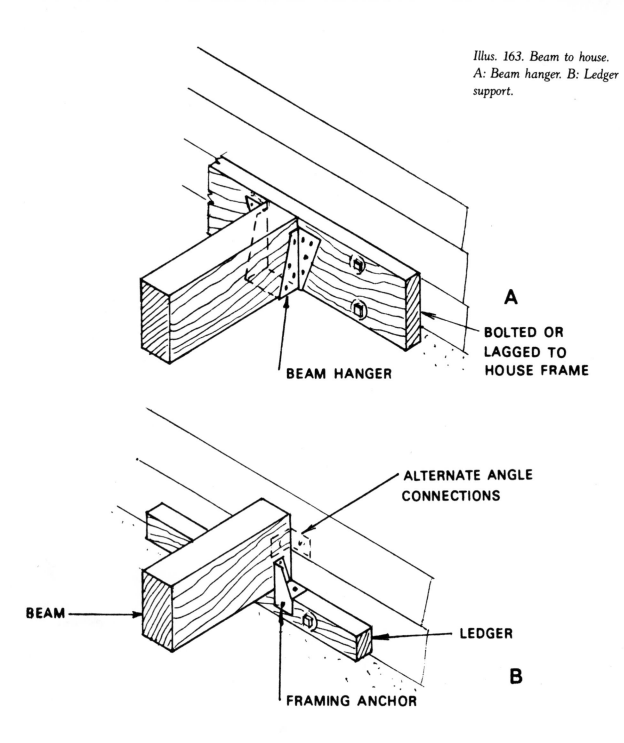

A

BOLTED OR LAGGED TO HOUSE FRAME

BEAM HANGER

ALTERNATE ANGLE CONNECTIONS

BEAM

LEDGER

B

FRAMING ANCHOR

tional bracing. However, when posts rest directly on concrete footings or pedestals, and unsupported heights are more than about 5 feet, some system of bracing should be used. Braces between adjacent posts serve the same purpose as bracing in the walls of a house.

Special bracing in the horizontal plane is normally not needed for residential decks of moderate area and height. Decks can be braced efficiently

Illus. 164. Joist to house.
A: Ledger support. B: Joist
hangers. C: Unconnected
joists.

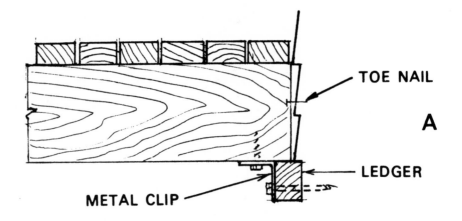

TOE NAIL

A

METAL CLIP

LEDGER

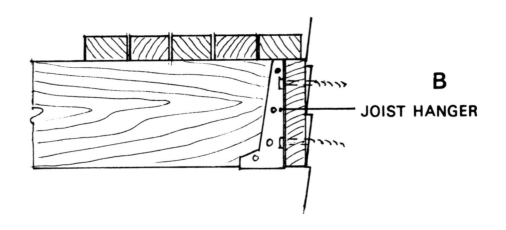

B

JOIST HANGER

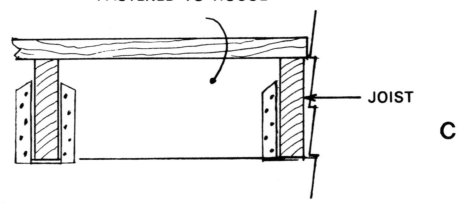

SUPPORTING MEMBER
FASTENED TO HOUSE

JOIST

C

in the horizontal plane by installing galvanized steel strap diagonals just under the deck surface. These should be in pairs in the direction of both diagonals and securely fastened at both ends. An alternative is to use flat 2- by 4-inch or 2- by 6-inch members across one diagonal, securely nailed to the underside of the deck members. In the case of a very large, high deck, it is advisable to consult a design engineer for an adequate bracing procedure.

Types of bracing Bracing should be used on each side of a "free" deck to provide racking resistance in each direction. Single bracing (one member per bay) should consist of 2-inch dimension material. When brace length is no greater than 8 feet, 2- by 4-inch members can be used; 2- by 6-inch bracers should be used when lengths are over 8 feet. Fastenings should normally consist of lag screws or bolts (with washers) to fasten 2-inch braces to the posts. See Fasteners section for proper fastener use.

One simple system of single bracing is known as the W-brace, which can be arranged as shown in Illus. 165A. Braces are lag-screwed to the post and joined along the centerline. When desired and when space is available, braces can be placed on the inside of the posts.

Another single bracing method between posts is shown in Illus. 165B. Braces are located from the base of one post to the top of the adjacent posts. Braces on the adjacent side of the deck should be placed in the opposite direction.

Another system of bracing used between posts is the X, or cross, brace (Illus. 165C). When spans and heights of posts are quite great, a cross brace can be used at each bay. However, bracing at alternate bays is normally sufficient. A bolt may be used where the 2-inch braces cross to further stabilize the bay. One-inch thick lumber bracing is not recommended as it is subject to mechanical damage such as splitting at the nails.

When posts are about 14 feet or more in height, which could occur on very steep slopes, two braces might be required to avoid the use of too long a brace. Such bracing can be arranged as shown in Illus. 165D.

Partial bracing A plywood gusset brace, or one made of short lengths of nominal 2-inch lumber, can sometimes be used as a partial brace for moderate post heights of 5 to 7 feet. A plywood gusset on each side of a post can also serve as a means of connection between a post and beam (Illus. 166A). Use ¾-inch exterior-type plywood and fasten to the post and beam with two rows of 10^d nails. The top edge of the gusset should be protected by an edge or header member that extends over the plywood.

A partial brace made of 2- by 4-inch lumber can be secured to the beam and posts with lag screws or bolts as shown in Illus. 166B. Some member of the deck, such as the deck boards or a parallel edge member, can overlap the upper ends to protect the end grain from moisture. When an overlap

*Illus. 165. Bracing. A: W-
brace. B: Single direction
brace. C: Cross brace.
D: Bracing for high posts.*

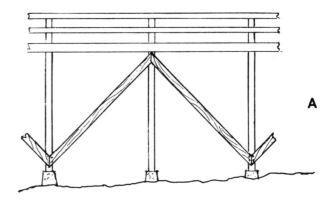

A

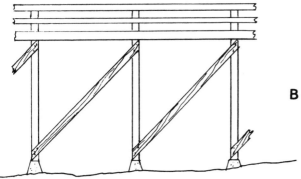

B

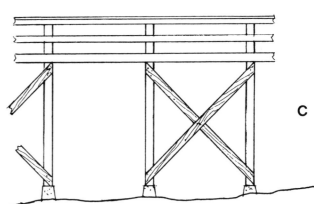

C

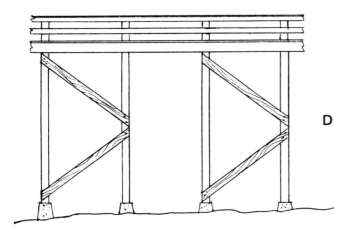

D

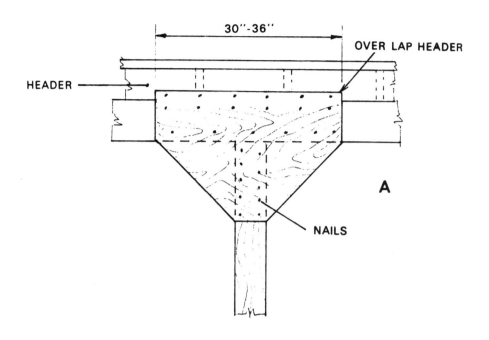

30"-36"

OVER LAP HEADER

HEADER

A

NAILS

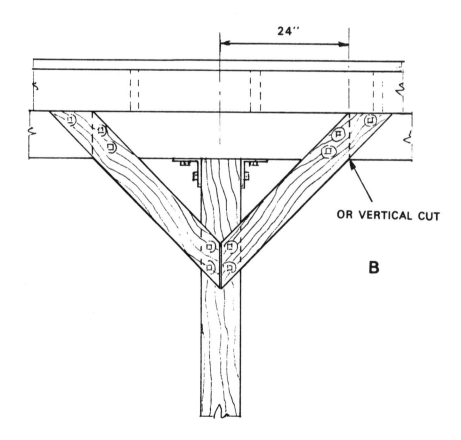

24"

OR VERTICAL CUT

B

member is not available and the area is sufficient for two fasteners, a vertical cut can be used for the brace.

Fastening braces Brace-to-post connections should be made to minimize trapped moisture or exposed end grain yet provide good resistance to any racking stresses. The detail in Illus. 167A has exposed end grain and should be avoided unless protected by an overlapping header or other member above. Illus. 167B shows a more acceptable cut. No end grain of the brace is exposed. Use two lag screws (or bolts) for 2- by 4-inch and 2- by 6-inch braces.

When two braces join at a post, such as occurs in a W-brace, connection should be made on the centerline as shown in Illus. 168A. A tight joint provides the resistance of all fasteners when one brace is in compression,

Illus. 167. Brace cuts.
A: Poor practice. B: Better practice.

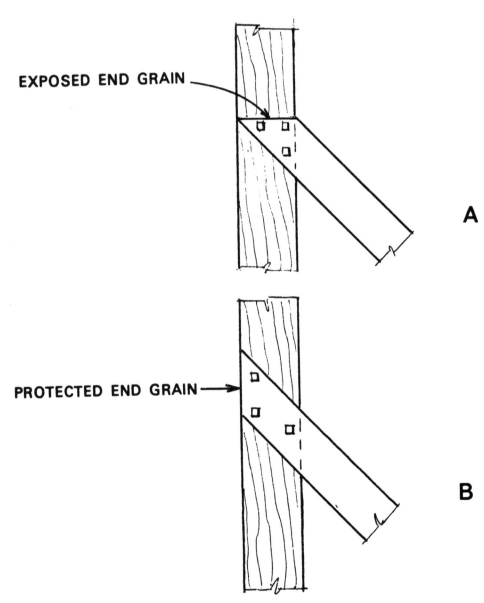

EXPOSED END GRAIN

A

PROTECTED END GRAIN

B

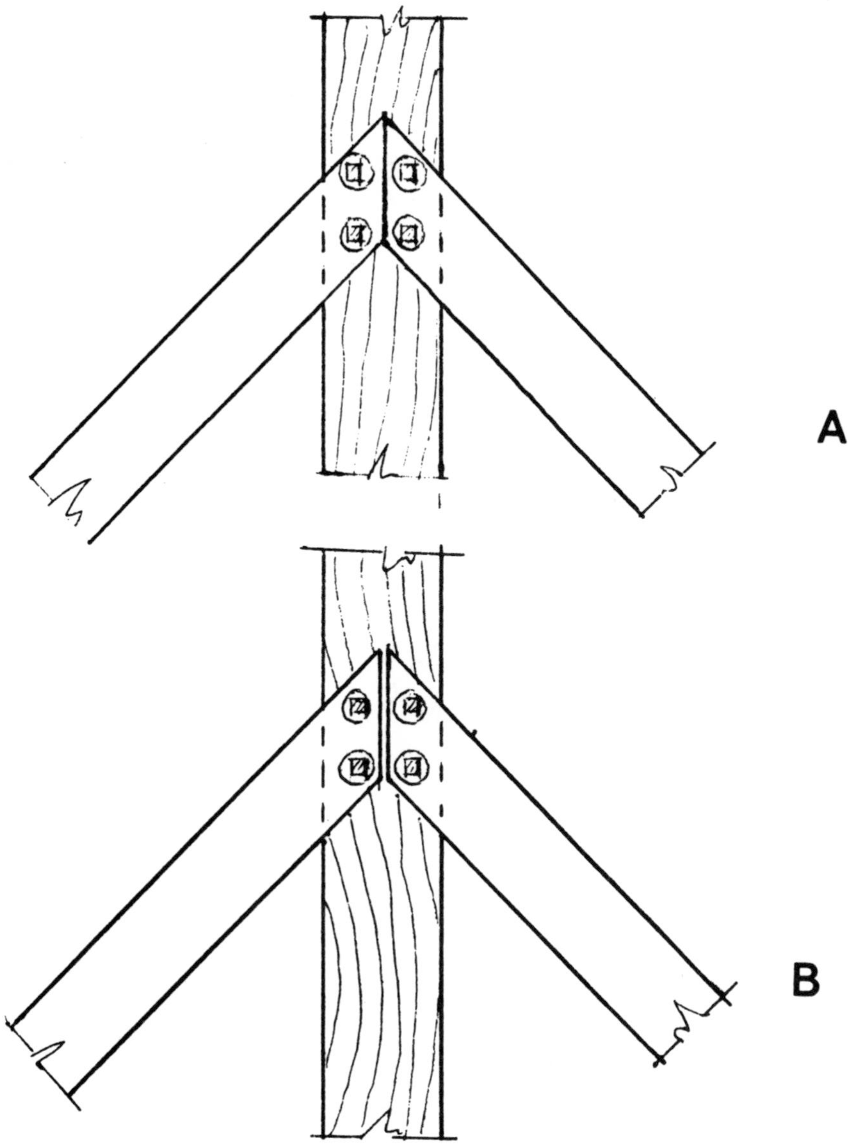

*Illus. 168. Joint at post.
A: Tight joint. B: Open joint
(preferred).*

A

B

but there is some hazard in trapped moisture. Illus. 168B shows a spaced joint, which is preferred when constant exposure to moisture is a factor.

A flush brace may be used if desired from the standpoint of appearance (Illus. 169). This type of connection requires that a backing cleat be lagged or bolted to each side of the post. The braces are then fastened to the cleats as shown.

The use of large, galvanized washers or other means of isolating the brace from the post will provide a smaller area for trapping moisture behind the brace (Illus. 170). Such a spacer at each bolt or lag screw might be used when the less decay-resistant wood species are involved.

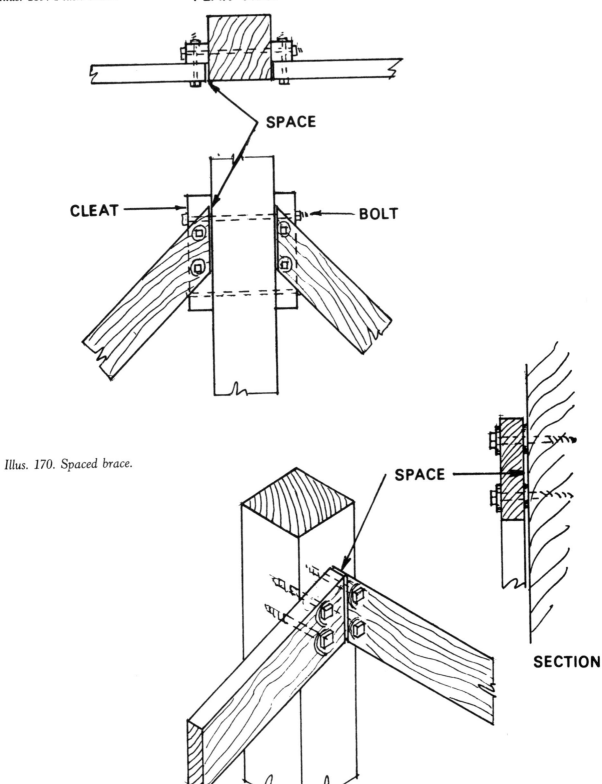

Illus. 169. Flush brace.

PLAN VIEW

SPACE

CLEAT → ← BOLT

Illus. 170. Spaced brace.

SPACE

SECTION

JOIST-TO-BEAM CONNECTIONS

When beams are spaced 2 to 5 feet apart and 2- by 4-inch Douglas fir or similar deck boards are used, there is no need to use joists to support the decking. The beams thus serve as both fastening and support members for the 2-inch deck boards. However, if the spans between beams are more than 3½ to 5 feet apart, it is necessary to use joists between the beams or 2 by 3 or 2 by 4 on edge for decking (see Table 4). To provide rigidity to the structure, the joists must be fastened to the beam in one of several ways. **Joists bearing directly on the beams** may be toe-nailed to the beam with one or two nails on each side (Illus. 171A). Use 10^d nails and avoid splitting. When uplift stresses are inclined to be great in high wind areas, supplementary metal strapping might be used in addition to the toe-nailing (Illus. 171B). Use 24- to 26-ga. galvanized strapping and nail with 1-inch galvanized roofing nails. When a header is used at the joist ends, nail the header into the end of each joist (Illus. 171C). Have the header overhang the beam by ½-inch to provide a good drip edge.

Joists located between beams and flush with their tops may be connected in two manners. One utilizes a 2- by 3-inch or 2- by 4-inch ledger that is spiked to the beam. Joists are cut between beams and toe-nailed to the beams at each end (Illus. 172A). The joint can be improved by the use of small metal clips.

Another method utilizes a metal joist hanger (Illus. 172B). The hanger is first nailed to the end of the joist with 1- to 1¼-inch galvanized roofing nails and then to the beam. Several types of joist hangers are available (Illus. 172C).

FASTENING DECK BOARDS

Deck boards are fastened to floor joists or to beams through their face with nails or screws. Screws are more costly to use than nails from the standpoint of material and labor but have greater resistance to loosening or withdrawal than the nail. A good compromise between the common smooth shank nail and the screw is the deformed shank nail (see Fasteners section). These nails retain their withdrawal resistance even under repeated wetting and drying cycles. Both nails and screws should be set flush or just below the surface of the deck board.

Some good rules in fastening deck boards to the joists or beams are as follows:

1. Number of fasteners per deck board: Use two fasteners for nominal 2- by 3-inch and 2- by 4-inch decking laid flat (Illus. 173A). For 2 by 3's or 2 by 4's on edge, use one fastener per joist (Illus. 173B).

Illus. 171. Joist-to-beam connection. A: Toe nail. B: Strapping. C: Connection with header.

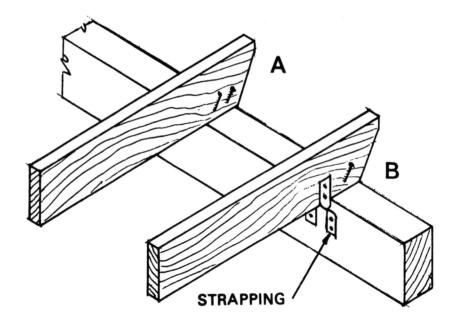

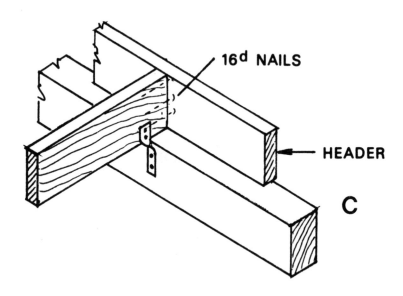

2. Size of fasteners:
   - Nails (deformed shank, galvanized, aluminum, etc.):
     - Nominal 2-inch thick deck boards—12^d,
     - Nominal 2- by 3-inch deck boards on edge—5 inches, and
     - Nominal 2- by 4-inch deck board (nailing not recommended).
   - Screws (flat or oval head, rust proof):
     - Nominal 2-inch thick deck boards—3 inch,

- Nominal 2- by 3-inch deck boards on edge—4½ inch, and
- Nominal 2- by 4-inch deck boards on edge—5 inch.

3. Spacing: Space all deck boards (flat or vertical) ⅛ to ¼-inch apart (use 8^d or 10^d nail for ⅛-inch spacing).

4. End joints (butt joints): End joints of flat deck boards should be made over the center of the joist or beam (Illus. 174A). In flat-grain boards, always place with the bark side up (Illus. 174B). When the upper face gets wet, it crowns slightly and water drains off more easily. End joints of any deck boards on edge should be made over a spaced double joist (Illus. 175A), a 4-inch or wider single beam, or a nominal 2-inch joist with nailing cleats on each side (Illus. 175B).

When deck boards are used on edge, spacers between runs will aid in maintaining uniform spacing and can be made to effect lateral support between runs by using lateral nailing at the spacers. Spacers as shown in Illus. 175C are recommended between supports when spans exceed 4 feet and should be placed so that no distance between supports or spacers

Illus. 172. Joists between beams. A: Ledger support. B: Joist hanger support. C: Joist hangers.

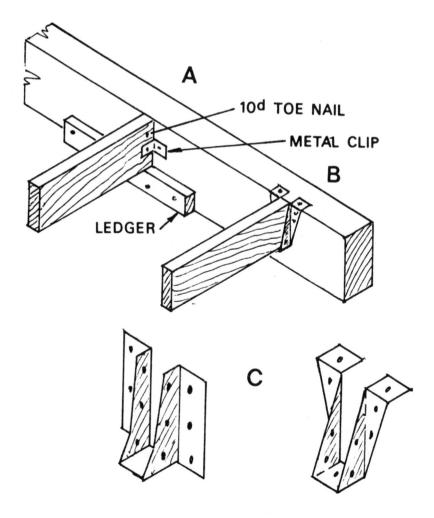

A

10^d TOE NAIL

METAL CLIP

B

LEDGER

C

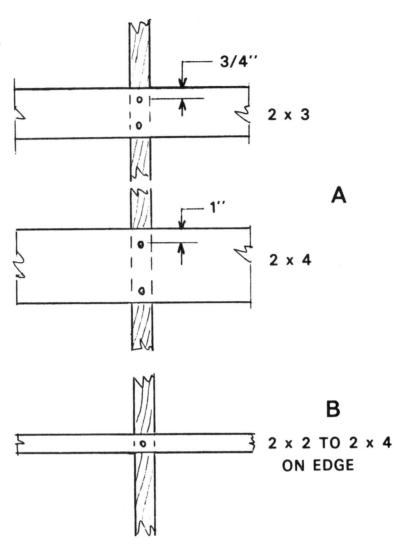

Illus. 173. Fastening deck boards. A: Flat deck boards. B: Deck boards on edge.

3/4''

2 x 3

A

1''

2 x 4

B

2 x 2 TO 2 x 4
ON EDGE

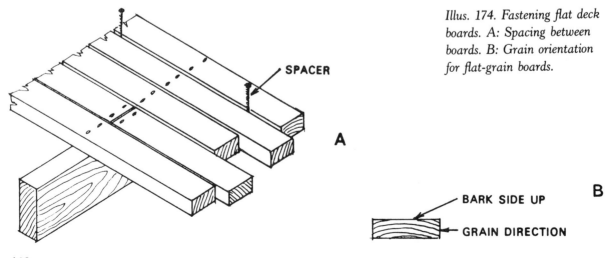

SPACER

A

Illus. 174. Fastening flat deck boards. A: Spacing between boards. B: Grain orientation for flat-grain boards.

B

BARK SIDE UP

GRAIN DIRECTION

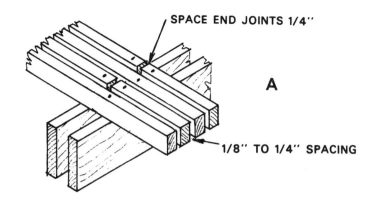

SPACE END JOINTS 1/4"

A

1/8" TO 1/4" SPACING

Illus. 175. Fastening "on edge" deck boards. A: Installing over double joist or beam. B: Installing over single joist or beam. C: Spacers for 2 × 4 decking on edge.

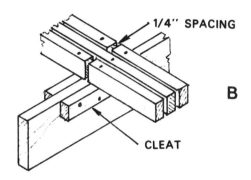

1/4" SPACING

B

CLEAT

1/8" x 3" x 3-1/2" TEMPERED HARDBOARD
SPACERS SET IN WATERPROOF CONSTRUCTION
ADHESIVE OR PENTA-GREASE

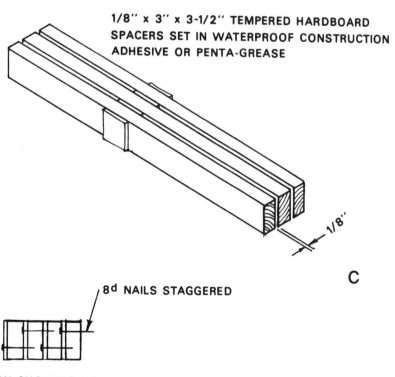

1/8"

C

8ᵈ NAILS STAGGERED

SECTION SHOWING NAILING

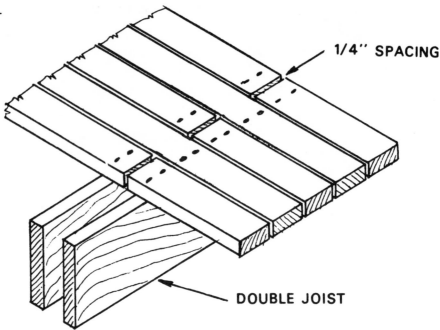

Illus. 176. End joints of decking over double joist.

1/4″ SPACING

DOUBLE JOIST

exceeds 4 feet. An elastomeric construction adhesive or penta-grease on both faces of each spacer prevents water retention in the joists.

Always dip ends of deck boards in water-repellent preservative before installing.

Always predrill ends of 2- by 3-inch or 2- by 4-inch (flat) deck boards of the denser species, or when there is a tendency to split. Predrill when screws are used for fastening. Predrill all fastening points of 2- by 3-inch or 2- by 4-inch deck boards placed on edge.

To provide longer useful life for decks made of low to moderate decay-resistant species, use one or more of the following precautions:

- Use spaced double joists or beams and place end joists between (Illus. 176).
- Lay a strip of building felt saturated with a wood preservative over the beam or joist before installing deck boards.
- Apply an elastomeric glue to the beam or joist edge before installing the deck boards.
- Treat end joints of deck boards made over a support with yearly applications of a water-repellent preservative. (A plunger-type oil can·will work well.)

FASTENING PLYWOOD

Plywood panels should generally be installed with a minimum ⅟₁₆-inch space between edge and end joints, using the support spacing and nailing schedule indicated in Table 6. When caulking is used, a joint space of at least ¼-inch is usually required.

To avoid unnecessary moisture absorption by the plywood, seal all panel edges with an exterior primer or an aluminum paint formulated for wood. The panel edge sealant can be most conveniently applied prior to installation, while the plywood is still in stacks. Build some slope into the deck area to provide for adequate drainage. A minimum slope of 1 inch in 8 to 10 feet should be provided when installing the joists or beams.

Provide ventilation for the underside of the deck areas in all cases. For low-level decks, this can be done by leaving the space between the joists open at the ends and by excavating material away from the support joists and beams. For high-level decks over enclosed areas, holes can be drilled in the blocking between joists.

RAILING POSTS

Low-level decks located just above the grade normally require no railings. However, if the site is sloped, some type of protective railing or system of balusters might be needed, because of the height of the deck.

The key members of a railing are the posts. Posts must be large enough and well fastened to provide strength to the railing. Some type of vertical member such as the post can also serve as a part of a bench or similar edge structure of the deck. Railings should be designed for a lateral load of at least 20 pounds per lineal foot. Thus, posts must be rigid and spaced properly to resist such loads.

One method of providing posts for the deck railing is by the extension of the posts that support the beams (Illus. 177). When single or double beams are fastened in this manner, the posts can extend above the deck floor and serve for fastening the railing and other horizontal members. Railing heights may vary between 30 and 40 inches, or higher when a bench or wind screen is involved. Posts should be spaced no more than 6 feet apart for a 2 by 4 horizontal top rail and 8 feet apart when a 2 by 6 or larger rail is used.

When supporting posts cannot be extended above the deck, a joist or beam may be available to which the posts can be secured. Posts can then be arranged as shown in Illus. 178A. Such posts can be made from 2 by 6's for spans less than 4 feet, from 4 by 4's or 2 by 8's for 4- to 6-foot spans, and from 4 by 6's or 3 by 8's for 6- to 8-foot spans. Each post should be bolted to the edge beam with two ⅜-inch or larger bolts determined by the size of the post. This system can also be used when the railing consists of a number of small baluster-type posts (Illus. 178B). When such posts are made of 2- by 2- or 2- by 3-inch members and spaced 12 to 16 inches apart,

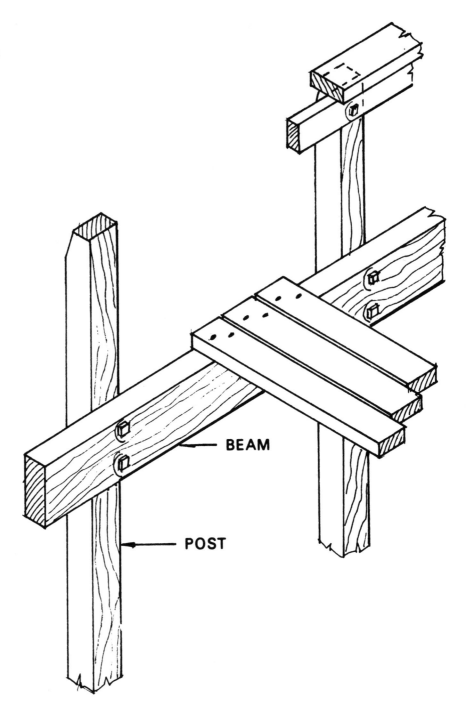

Illus. 177. Extension of post to serve as a railing support.

BEAM

POST

the top fastener into the beam should be a ¼- or ⅜-inch bolt or lag screw. The bottom fastener can then be a 12^d or larger deformed shank nail. Predrill when necessary to prevent splitting. Wider spacings or larger size posts require two bolts. A ⅛-inch to ¼-inch space should be allowed between the ends of floor boards and posts.

The ends of beams or joists along the edge of the deck can also be used to fasten the railing posts. One such fastening system is shown in Illus. 179.

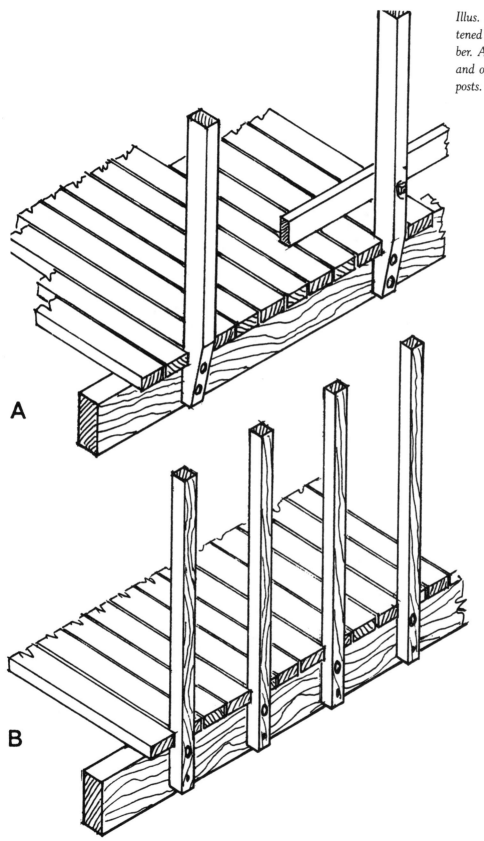

Illus. 178. Railing posts fastened to edge of deck member. A: Spaced posts (4 feet and over). B: Baluster-type posts.

A

B

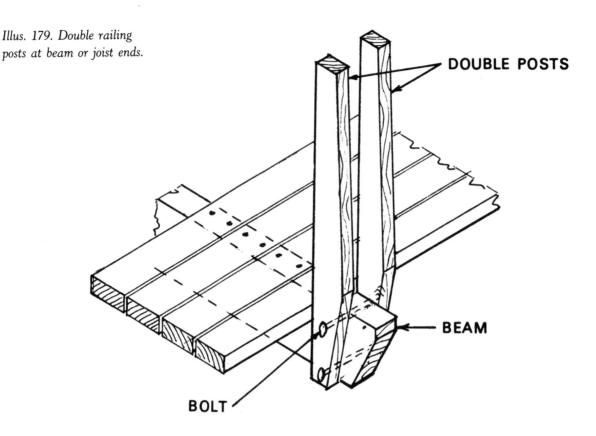

Illus. 179. Double railing posts at beam or joist ends.

DOUBLE POSTS

BEAM

BOLT

Single or double (one on each side) posts are bolted to the ends of the joists or beams. Space the bolts as far apart as practical for better lateral resistance.

The practice of mounting posts on a deck board should be avoided. Not only is the railing structurally weak, but the bottom of the post has end grain contact with a flat surface. This could induce high moisture content and possible decay.

DECK BENCHES

High-deck benches At times there is an advantage in using a bench along the edge of a high deck, combining utility with protection. One such design is shown in Illus. 180. The vertical back supporting members (bench posts), spaced no more than 6 feet apart, are bolted to the beams. They can also be fastened to extensions of the floor joists. When beams are more than 6 feet apart, the bench post can be fastened to an edge joist in much the same manner as railing posts. The backs and seat supports should be spaced no more than 6 feet apart when nominal 2-inch plank seats are used.

Low-deck benches Benches can also be used along the edge of low decks.

These can be simple plank seats that serve as a backdrop for the deck. Such bench seats require vertical members fastened to the joists or beams with cross cleats (Illus. 181). For nominal 2-inch plank seats, vertical supports should be bolted to a joist or beam and be spaced no more than 6 feet apart. A single wide support (2 by 10) (Illus. 181A) or double (two 2 by 4's) supports (Illus. 181B) can be used. Cleats should be at least 2 by 3 inches in size.

Such member arrangements can also be used as a step between two decks with elevation differences of 12 to 16 inches. Many other bench arrangements are possible; but spans, fastenings, and elimination of end-grain exposure should always be considered.

Illus. 180. Deck bench.

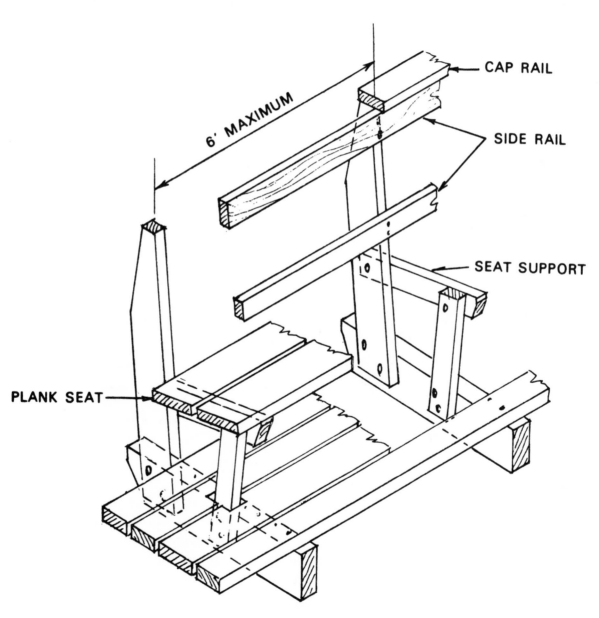

Illus. 181. Bench seats.
A: Single support and cross
cleat. B: Double support.

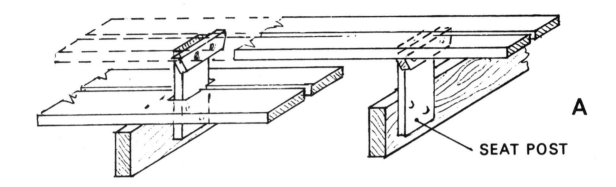

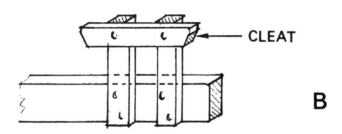

RAILINGS

Horizontal railings The top horizontal members of a railing should be arranged to protect the end grain of vertical members such as posts or balusters. A poorly designed railing detail is shown in Illus. 182. Such details should be avoided, as the end grain of the baluster-type posts is exposed. Illus. 183 is an improvement, as the end grain of the balusters is protected by the cap rail.

The upper side rail, which is usually a 2- by 4-inch or wider member, should be fastened to the posts with a lag screw or bolt at each crossing. The cap rail then can be nailed to the edge of the top rail with 12^d deformed shank nails spaced 12 to 16 inches apart.

When railing posts are spaced more than about 2 feet apart, additional horizontal members may be required as a protective barrier. These side rails should be nominal 2- by 4-inch members when posts are spaced no more than 4 feet apart. Use 2 by 6s when posts are spaced over 4 feet apart.

Rail fastenings When the upper side rail is bolted to the post (Illus. 184), the remaining rails can be nailed to the posts. Use two 12^d deformed shank nails at each post and splice side rails and all horizontal members at the centerline of a post. Posts must be more than 2 inches in thickness to provide an adequate fastening area at each side of the center splice.

A superior rail termination consists of the use of a double post (Illus. 185). Horizontal members are spaced about 1 inch apart, which allows ends of members to dry quickly after rains. As in all wood deck members, the ends should always be dipped in water-repellent preservative before assembly.

Cap rail connections A good method of fastening cap rail to the post has been shown in the previous section and in Illus. 183. In some designs, however, the cap rail without additional members may be specified. An unsatisfactory method of connecting a cap rail to the post is by nailing (Illus. 186A). End-grain nailing is not recommended in such connections. A better method is shown in Illus. 186B. Short lengths of galvanized angle irons are fastened to the post with lag screws or bolts. The cap rail is then fastened with short (1½-inch) lag screws. Although this is certainly not as simple as nailing, it provides an excellent joint and fastenings are not exposed to the weather.

Miscellaneous rail connections There may be occasions in the construc-

Illus. 182. Poorly designed railing detail.

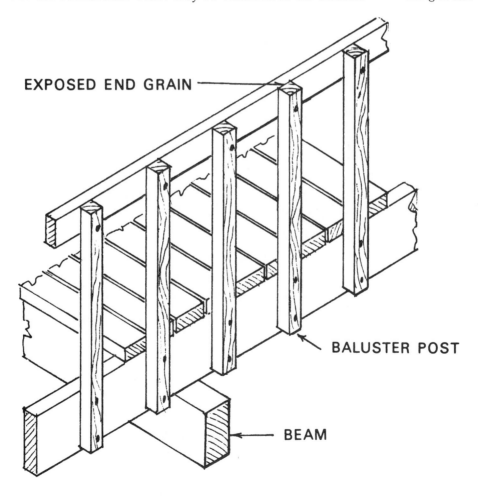

EXPOSED END GRAIN

BALUSTER POST

BEAM

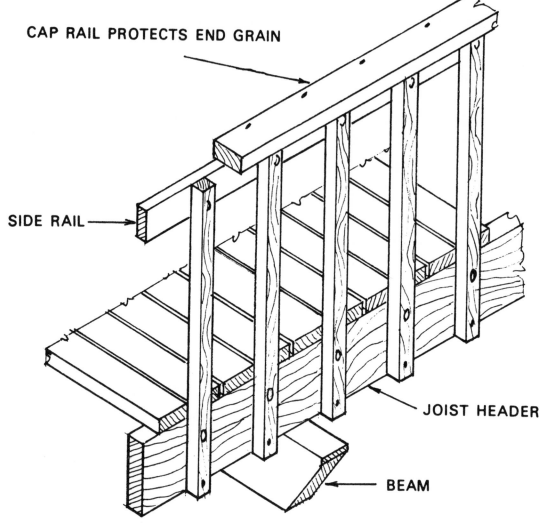

CAP RAIL PROTECTS END GRAIN

SIDE RAIL

JOIST HEADER

BEAM

tion of a railing of a deck to use members between the posts rather than lapping the posts. This might be in construction of an adjoining wind screen or midheight railings between posts. Such connections might also be adaptable to fences where horizontal members are located between posts. The connection to the post is the important one, as it must be rigid as well as minimize areas where moisture could be trapped. Dado cuts for a 2-inch rail are shown in Illus. 187A and 187B. Although these are reasonably good structurally, moisture could be retained at the end grain of the bottom cut. Illus. 187C shows the notch reversed. This will not retain moisture as much as the previous cuts, but the member must be cut precisely to provide a rigid joint. A wood block lag-screwed to the side of the post serves as a good fastening area for the rail (Illus. 187D). This is a good connection when the rail is spaced slightly away from the post. The rails should be fastened to the block with screws.

A commercial-type bracket is shown in Illus. 187E. This connector can also be used to advantage for 1-inch members used in a fence or a wind screen. Another good method utilizes a small angle iron lagged to the post (Illus. 187F). The rail is then fastened to the angle with lag screws from below.

STAIRWAYS

There is often a need for a stairway as an access to a deck or for use between decks with different levels. Exterior stairs are much the same as

Illus. 184. Side rails for deck railing.

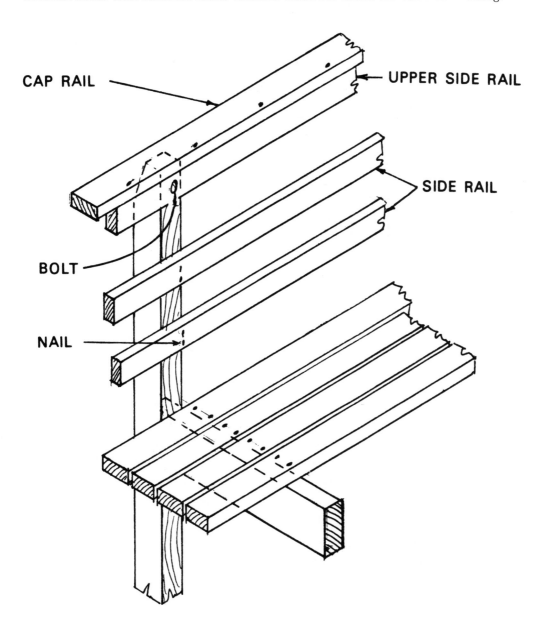

CAP RAIL

UPPER SIDE RAIL

SIDE RAIL

BOLT

NAIL

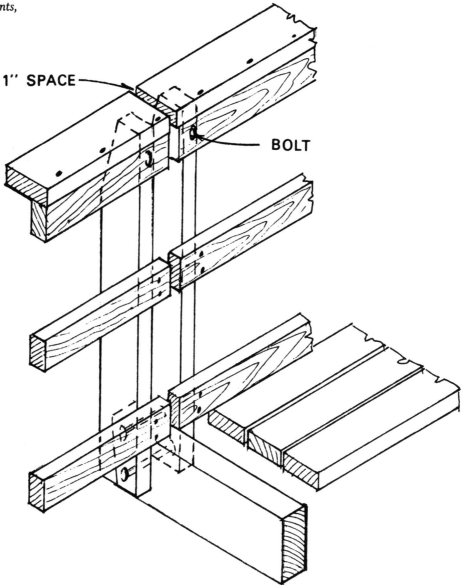

1" SPACE

BOLT

stairs within a house, except that details which avoid trapped moisture or exposed end grain of the members should be used.

Research has indicated that for woods with moderate to low decay resistance, a three-minute dip in a water-repellent preservative for all members at least tripled the average service life of exterior stairways and their parts. Use of all-heartwood of decay-resistant species or of pressure-treated wood will insure even longer life.

Stair stringers A basic stair consists of stair stringer (sometimes called stair carriage) and treads. Additional parts include balusters and side cap rails and, on occasion, risers. The supporting members of a stair are the stringers. Stringers are used in pairs spaced no more than 3 feet apart. They are usually made of 2- by 10-inch or 2- by 12-inch members. Stringers must be well secured to the framing of the deck. They are normally supported by a ledger or by the extension of a joist or beam. A 2- by 3-inch or 2- by 4-inch ledger nailed to the bottom of an edge framing member with 12^d nails supports the notched stringer (Illus. 188A). Toe-nailing or small metal clips are used to secure the carriage in place. Stair stringers can also be bolted to the ends of joists or beams when they are spaced no more than about 3 feet apart (Illus. 188B). Use at least two ½-inch galvanized bolts to fasten the stringer to the beam or joist.

The bottom of the stair stringers should be anchored to a solid base and be isolated from any moisture source. Two systems frequently used consist of metal angles anchored to a concrete base (Illus. 189A and 189B). The angles should be thick enough to raise the stringer off the concrete, which

Illus. 186. Fastening cap rail to post. A: Nailed (end grain), a poor practice. B: Angle iron connection, a good practice.

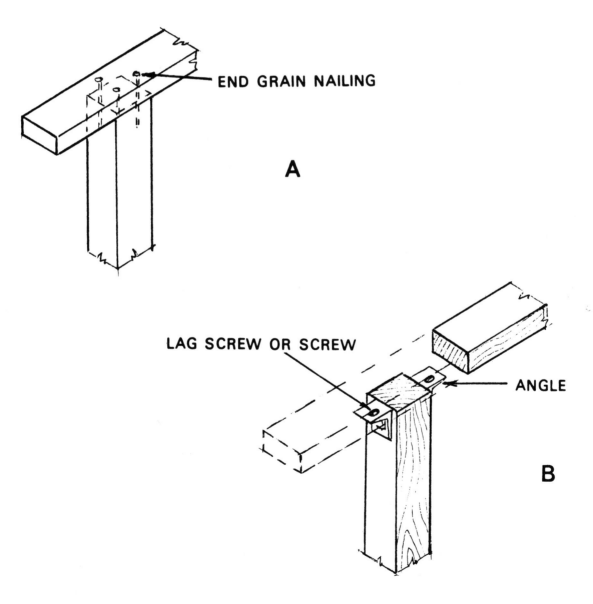

END GRAIN NAILING

A

LAG SCREW OR SCREW

ANGLE

B

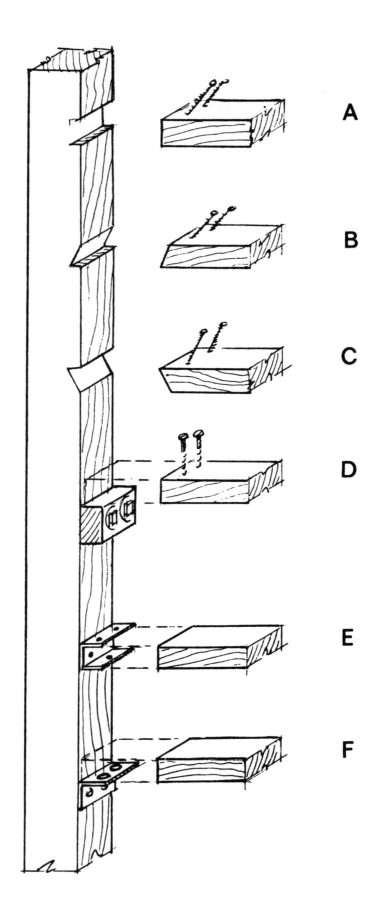

Illus. 187. Rail-to-post connections. A–C: Dado cuts (not recommended). D: Wood block support. E: Metal connector. F: Angle iron.

A

B

C

D

E

F

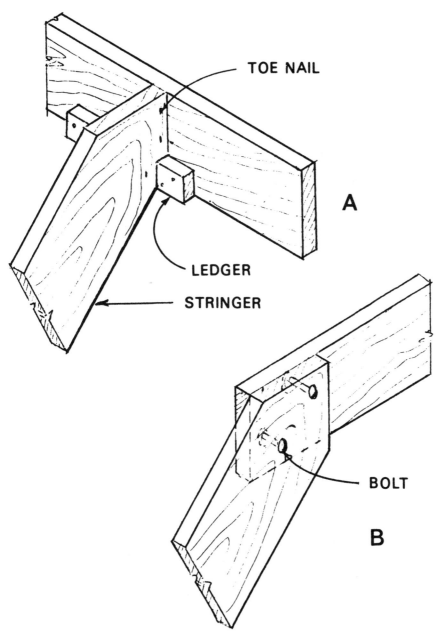

TOE NAIL

A

LEDGER

STRINGER

BOLT

B

should also be sloped for drainage. They might also be fastened to a treated wood member anchored in the concrete or in the ground.

Tread and riser size The relation of the tread width (run) to the riser height is important in determining the number of steps required. For ease of ascent, the rise of each step in inches times the width of the tread in inches should equal 72 to 75 (Illus. 190A). Thus, if the riser is 8 inches (considered maximum for stairs), the tread would be 9 inches. Or if the riser is 7½ inches, the tread should be about 10 inches. Thus the number of risers and treads can be found when the total height of the stair is known. Divide total

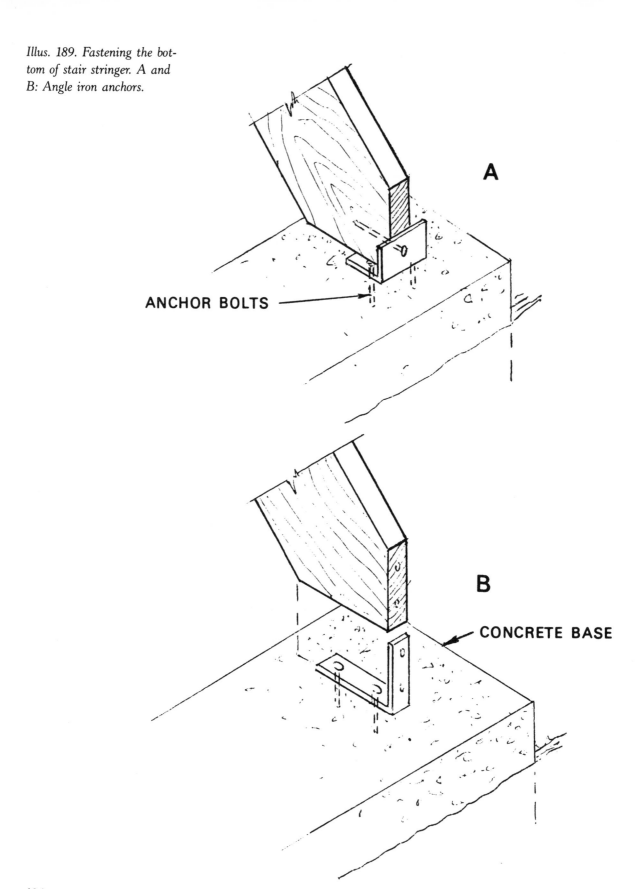

Illus. 189. Fastening the bottom of stair stringer. A and B: Angle iron anchors.

A

ANCHOR BOLTS ⟶

B

⟵ CONCRETE BASE

rise in inches by 7½ (each riser) and select the nearest whole number. Thus, if the total rise is 100 inches, the number of risers would be 13 and the total run, about 120 inches (Illus. 190B).

Tread support Stair treads can be supported by dadoes cut into the stringer (Illus. 191A). Stringers can also be notched to form supports for the tread and riser (Illus. 191B). However, both methods introduce end-grain exposure and possible trapped moisture and should be avoided for exposed stairs, especially when untreated, low decay-resistant species are used.

Illus. 190. Riser-to tread relationship. A: Individual step. B: Total rise and run.

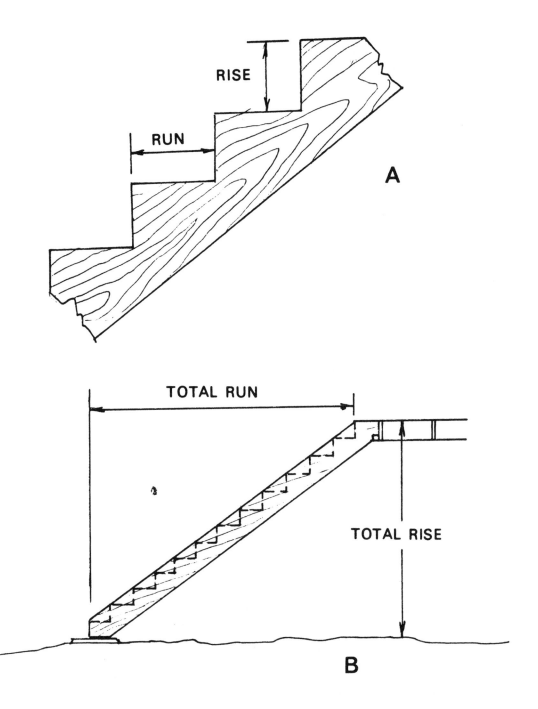

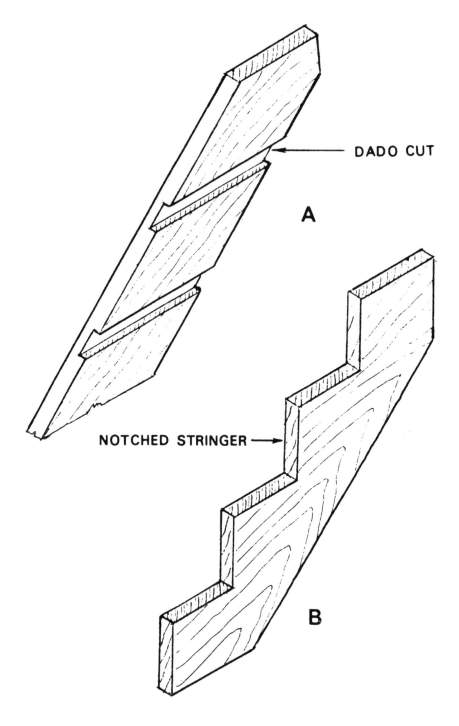

Illus. 191. Tread supports, not recommended. A: Dadoed stringer, poor practice. B: Notched, better practice.

DADO CUT

A

NOTCHED STRINGER →

B

A better method of tread support consists of 2- by 4-inch ledgers or cleats bolted to the stair stringers and extended to form supports for the plank treads (Illus. 192A). The ledgers can be sloped back slightly so that rain will drain off the treads. Ledgers might also be beveled slightly to minimize tread contact. Nail 2- by 10-inch or 2- by 12-inch treads to the ledgers with three 12^d deformed shank nails at each stringer. Rust-proof

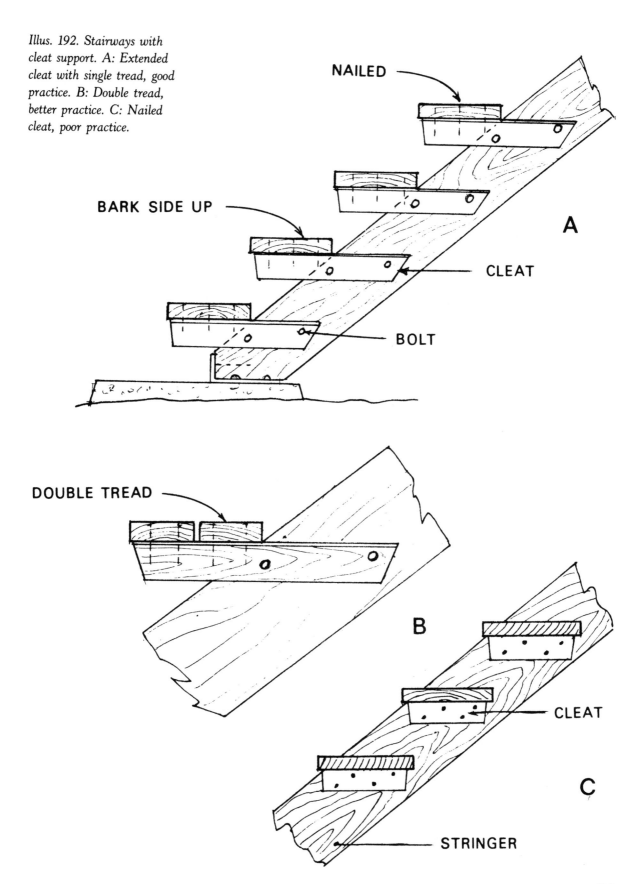

Illus. 192. Stairways with cleat support. A: Extended cleat with single tread, good practice. B: Double tread, better practice. C: Nailed cleat, poor practice.

NAILED

BARK SIDE UP

CLEAT

BOLT

A

DOUBLE TREAD

B

CLEAT

C

STRINGER

wood screws 3 inches in length can also be used. Always place plank treads with bark side-up to prevent cupping and retention of rain water. Treads can also be made of two 2- by 6-inch planks, but the span must be limited to 42 inches for the less-dense woods (Illus. 192B).

Another method of fastening the stair cleats is by nailing them directly to the stair stringers. Use 2- by 3-inch or 2- by 4-inch cleats and fasten with three or four 12[d] deformed shank nails. Treads are then nailed to the cleats in a normal manner. This method is not as resistant to exposure as the extended cleat shown in Illus. 192A, because there are more areas for trapped moisture. However, with the use of a decay-resistant species and water-repellent preservative treatment, good service should result.

Stair railings On moderate to full height stairs with one or both sides unprotected, some type of railing is advisable. Railings for stairs are constructed much the same as railings for the deck. In fact, from the standpoint of appearance, they should have the same design. Railings normally consist of posts fastened to stair stringers and supplementary members, such as top and intermediate rails.

Illus. 193. Widely spaced stair posts.

One method similar to a deck rail uses widely spaced posts and protective railings (Illus. 193). Posts are 2- by 4-inch members when spacing is no

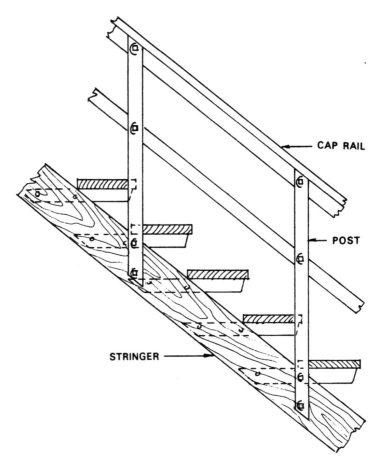

CAP RAIL

POST

STRINGER

more than 3 feet and 3- by 4-inch or 2- by 6-inch members for spacings from 3 to 6 feet. Longitudinal cap rails, top and intermediate, are normally 2- by 4-inch or wider members. Assembly should be with bolts or lag screws. The cap rail can be nailed to the top rail with 12^d deformed shank nails spaced 12 to 16 inches apart.

The design shown in Illus. 194 has closely spaced posts which serve as

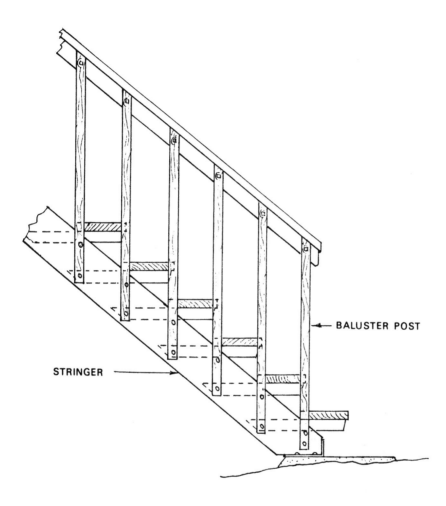

Illus. 194. Baluster-type stair posts.

BALUSTER POST

STRINGER

balusters. Each should be bolted to the stringer and to a top rail. The cap rail, which also protects the baluster ends, can then be nailed to the adjoining rail.

A single cap railing can also be used for such stairs, but it is advisable to fasten it to the posts with metal clips or angles to eliminate unreliable end-grain fastening.

Many other variations of post and rail combination can be used. All designs should consider safety and utility as well as a pleasing appearance. A well-designed deck, railing and stairway combination with care in details will provide years of pleasure with little maintenance.

METRIC EQUIVALENCY CHART

UNIT	ABBREVIATION		APPROXIMATE U.S. EQUIVALENT		
Length					
		Number of Metres			
myriametre	mym	10,000	6.2 miles		
kilometre	km	1000	0.62 mile		
hectometre	hm	100	109.36 yards		
dekametre	dam	10	32.81 feet		
metre	m	1	39.37 inches		
decimetre	dm	0.1	3.94 inches		
centimetre	cm	0.01	0.39 inch		
millimetre	mm	0.001	0.04 inch		
Area					
		Number of Square Metres			
square kilometre	sq km *or* km²	1,000,000	0.3861 square miles		
hectare	ha	10,000	2.47 acres		
are	a	100	119.60 square yards		
centare	ca	1	10.76 square feet		
square centimetre	sq cm *or* cm²	0.0001	0.155 square inch		
Volume					
		Number of Cubic Metres			
dekastere	das	10	13.10 cubic yards		
stere	s	1	1.31 cubic yards		
decistere	ds	0.10	3.53 cubic feet		
cubic centimetre	cu cm *or* cm³ *also* cc	0.000001	0.061 cubic inch		
Capacity					
		Number of Litres	*Cubic*	*Dry*	*Liquid*
kilolitre	kl	1000	1.31 cubic yards		
hectolitre	hl	100	3.53 cubic feet	2.84 bushels	
dekalitre	dal	10	0.35 cubic foot	1.14 pecks	2.64 gallons
litre	l	1	61.02 cubic inches	0.908 quart	1.057 quarts
decilitre	dl	0.10	6.1 cubic inches	0.18 pint	0.21 pint
centilitre	cl	0.01	0.6 cubic inch		0.338 fluidounce
millilitre	ml	0.001	0.06 cubic inch		0.27 fluidram
Mass and Weight					
		Number of Grams			
metric ton	MT *or* t	1,000,000	1.1 tons		
quintal	q	100,000	220.46 pounds		
kilogram	kg	1,000	2.2046 pounds		
hectogram	hg	100	3.527 ounces		
dekagram	dag	10	0.353 ounce		
gram	g *or* gm	1	0.035 ounce		
decigram	dg	0.10	1.543 grains		
centigram	cg	0.01	0.154 grain		
milligram	mg	0.001	0.015 grain		

PICTURE CREDITS

The editors and publishers wish to thank the following people and organizations for illustrations which they supplied:

Allied Tube & Conduit Corporation, Illus. 98, 99, 104–116; American Plywood Association, Illus. 31, 32; Black & Decker, Illus. 83; courtesy of California Redwood Association*, Illus. 4, 5, 8, 14, 17, 19, 23, 26, 36, 40, 42, 58, 120, 121, 123, 125, and all photographs in color section; Koppers Company, Illus. 3, 6, 9, 10, 15, 16, 18, 20–22, 24, 25, 34, 35, 37–39, 44, 48, 49, 97, 100–102, 117, 118, 122, 129, 130, 134; Porter Cable, Illus. 74; Steve Raynis, Illus. 11, 12, 27–30, 33, 45, 47, 51, 61, 136–139; Sears Roebuck & Company, Illus. 50, 75, 79; Shopsmith, Inc., Illus. 72; Stanley Tools, Illus. 71, 81, 82, 86.

All other illustrations in the section on fences and gates by Charles R. Self.

*Georgia-Pacific Corporation, Harwood Products Company, Miller Redwood Company, The Pacific Lumber Company, Simpson Timber Company, Timber Realization Company

Index